Popular Music

Popular Music

JOHN RUBLOWSKY

BASIC BOOKS, INC.,
PUBLISHERS
New York   London

SECOND PRINTING

© 1967 by John Rublowsky

Library of Congress Catalog Card Number: 67–28387

Manufactured in the United States of America

Designed by Loretta Li

TO DEAR OLD DAD
—*a pop musician from the old country*

CONTENTS

Popular Music

1 MAKING THE LISTS

> The hi-fi changeover was for music what cubism had been for painting and what symbolism had been for literature; namely, the acceptance of multiple facets and planes in a single experience. . . . When a medium becomes a depth experience the old categories of "classical" and "popular" or of "highbrow" and "lowbrow" no longer obtain.
>
> MARSHALL McLUHAN
> *Understanding Media*

A friend who vacationed in Europe recently came home with this story to tell. During his stay abroad, he traveled through Sicily and spent a day and night in a remote village in the interior of the island where motor scooters had not yet completely shouldered the donkeys and pony carts from its narrow, cobbled streets. That night he stopped for supper at a village café that turned out to be a local hangout for the younger set. As the evening wore on, the café filled with young men and teen-age boys—girls, our friend noted, were conspicuous by their absence—who listened and danced to sounds coming from what looked suspiciously like a big, gaudy Seeburg jukebox.

The machine held about fifty selections, most of them featuring Italian singers and musicians. These, however, were not what the local swains had gathered to hear. The only records played that night, according to our friend, were the three or four American rock-and-roll selections that had found their way to this distant corner of Sicily.

The story was offered as one more symptom of the general "ruin" of Europe—at least as far as this American tourist was concerned. Imagine having to listen to the strident blare of rock-and-roll in the soft, lemon-scented Sicilian night—on an American jukebox!

What our friend neglected to mention (in his haste to condemn) was that nobody made these young Sicilians play those particular records. They willingly gave up their coins—hard-earned in this corner of the world—to listen to music they wanted to hear. In so doing, they were showing their appreciation of that peculiar American genius whose creation has dominated the world's popular music for at least the past hundred years. They were responding to the all but universal appeal of popular American music.

It is difficult to isolate the factors responsible for the undeniable appeal of rock-and-roll. Musical analysis offers no help at all. For the most part, the rhythms are basic and obvious, the harmonies simple, and the lyrics—even for those of us who can understand them—are generally inane.

Yet there is a quality in this music that enables it to span oceans, to bridge the deepest cultural chasms, and to focus, as in this case, on the humanity shared by these young Sicilians with their counterparts in Chicago, Los Angeles, and Brooklyn. This music communicates on a wavelength that all understand and respond to. With rock-

and-roll, the whole, in defiance of mathematical convention, adds up to more than the sum of the parts.

Nor is this appeal confined to Italy, or even Europe for that matter. Popular American music has won an enthusiastic audience in practically every corner of the globe. In Japan, a thriving cult of Americana has evolved around the imported sounds from Tin Pan Alley. In Russia, bootlegged Elvis Presley records, taped from Voice of America broadcasts, command a premium price on the black market and are passed carefully from hand to hand as rare cultural treasures. In Lebanese nighteries, black-eyed houris doing the traditional belly dance are being replaced by Go-Go girls doing the frug. England's principal export, or so it might appear, is rapidly becoming music—music derived frankly from American sources.

The popularity of rock-and-roll represents only the most recent international invasion of American music. Similar crazes have gripped the world in the past. During the mid-nineteenth century, long before the era of the radio and phonograph record, the minstrel show was America's chief cultural export. Black-faced performers toured the world to enthrall audiences wherever they performed with their catchy tunes and broad humor.

No less a personage than England's august Queen Victoria responded to the minstrels' vitality and exuberance, while William Makepeace Thackeray, the English novelist, was so moved by a performance of Dan Bryant's Original Minstrel Show that he described Bryant's impersonation of the hungry old Negro in "Old Time Rocks" as "one of the finest pieces of tragic acting" that he knew.

At the turn of the century American ragtime was all

the rage. It had its roots in the minstrel show's flamboyant cakewalk and was spawned in the honky-tonks of St. Louis and Memphis, where Negro pianists developed, with freedom and originality, the style that was to be called ragtime. It spread from the South and rose rapidly to immense popularity both in America and abroad. This craze, which approached the current rock-and-roll reaction in intensity, saw the fox trot replace the waltz as the favorite ballroom dance. Ragtime also came to the attention of European composers, who were delighted with the freedom and vitality of the form. Claude Debussy, Anton Dvořák, and Camille Saint-Saëns were among the eminent musicians who utilized ragtime rhythms in their compositions—and at a time when "serious" musicians in America had nothing but contempt for this "barbaric" outpouring from the dregs of American society.

After World War I, American jazz spread abroad. The whole world began to beat its feet to the syncopated rhythms and improvisational inventions of New Orleans. Jazz came into being, essentially, when Negro musicians were able to obtain conventional manufactured instruments. By switching from banjo and bones to the trumpet, the cornet, the clarinet, the trombone, and the snare and bass drum, the range of musical expression was correspondingly broadened. This broadened range, in turn, demanded a new musical idiom.

What began as marching bands soon encompassed ragtime, blues, work songs, dance tunes, and gradually evolved into the expressive, syncopated, improvisational idiom known generically as Dixieland jazz. It developed in small bands during the 1890's and drew on the musical originality of such pioneers as Charles Bolden, "Bunk" Johnson, Freddie Keppard, Sidney Bechet, and "King" Oliver.

Unlike ragtime, this new jazz was quickly recognized as an important cultural contribution. European composers again were the earliest champions, and such figures as Stravinsky, Prokofiev, Milhaud, Ravel, and Satie came under the influence of this vigorous new music.

Today, rock-and-roll has taken possession of stage center.

Oddly enough, this universal popularity is hardly a source of pride for many Americans—especially for the older and the so-called "literate" portion of the population. Instead, it is a source of embarrassment. Self-appointed critics, forgetting the lessons of the past, have labeled rock-and-roll "vulgar," "tasteless," "crude," "cheap," "dumb," "primitive," "degrading," "uninspired"—adjectives, incidentally, that greeted both ragtime and jazz at their inception. These same critics then go on to protest that they, of course, *never listen to such trash.*

Obviously, there is a serious discrepancy between critical and public acceptance of this type of popular music. The problem may center on the fact that popular music is both an art form and a big business. As an art form, it provides the principal aesthetic experience for millions of people, especially teen-agers. As a business, its guiding principle, like that of every business, is profit. The two functions have become hopelessly confused.

This confusion is made possible, even inevitable, for the simple reason that business considerations do affect creation in the popular-music industry. More so, perhaps, than in other art forms. Still, no art is created in a vacuum, and commercial considerations have always been a primary influence. The old masters of the sixteenth century, for example, painted numerous portraits of dukes, kings, and wealthy merchants. Perhaps the sight of an important burgher inspired these artists. More likely the portraits came into being because these were the people who could pay to have them painted.

Most of our string quartets, a repertoire that includes some of the finest music ever written, came into being as the result of commercial transactions. They were composed because some obscure count or banker enjoyed playing the violin and wanted music to perform with a few close friends.

In popular music the relationship between commerce and art is even more obvious. Business considerations, for example, are directly responsible for the duplication and imitation that plague the industry. Should an innovation prove successful—that is, should it *sell*—it is followed immediately by dozens of imitations in the hope of capturing part of what appears to be a proven market.

At the same time, business considerations tend to inhibit innovation and experiment. The process was described succinctly by Irving Spice, an independent record producer: "You take a disk to a big distributor. He'll listen to it and say, 'Sorry, I can't take a chance on this side. Nobody's done anything like it before. How do I know how it's going to move?' Then that same distributor will listen to another side and say in his very next breath, 'No, that's not for me. Too imitative. Sounds like everything else on the market today.' "

Business and creative functions are so closely united that many people consider popular music an artificially created commodity, a commodity that has been rammed down our throats only through recourse to the most cynical kinds of manipulation and exploitation. This opinion appears to have been confirmed by the highly publicized "payola" scandals. Disk jockeys, investigation revealed, were accepting payments from record companies and music publishers for playing their material on their programs. This revelation was taken as positive proof that the popular-music industry was nothing more than a calculated manipulation of popular taste.

This view holds that the public is so gullible that it will buy anything provided enough effort is made in its exploitation. Perhaps there is an element of truth in this outlook, but it is doubtful that the Ford Motor Company would accept it after its experience with the Edsel, and it would be impossible to convince a harried A. and R. (Artists and Repertoire) executive who has carefully packaged a record, watched a sizable fortune in promotion money evaporate, and then seen his product flop dismally. It is estimated that 95 per cent of all records produced are flops despite the same frantic promotion that propels the remaining 5 per cent to success.

Investigations and uproar notwithstanding, payola still exists in the music business as it does in every other business. One of these days an enterprising reporter will expose the payola prevalent in classical music. The descriptions of the secret deals, the unsavory arrangements, and the payoffs that occur will make hair-raising reading, but they will not detract from the value of the product produced. Bach and Beethoven will emerge unscathed.

All this is by way of saying: "You can fool some of the people all of the time, and all of the people some of the time, but you can't fool all of the people all of the time."

The fact remains that payola never could and never will

be able to guarantee a hit record. Nor can it catapult any kid-off-the-street into national acclaim. Payola is like advertising in that it guarantees exposure of a particular product. The rest is up to the public, which makes the final decision.

And pleasing the public is what the popular-music industry is geared to do. Or, as Marty Manning, one of our leading arrangers whom we shall meet in a later chapter, puts it: "If the public wants stripes, we're not going to give them plaids."

Nor is this statement as cynical as it might appear at first glance. The function of an arranger of popular music is to produce a sound that will appeal to the broadest possible audience. All of his talents and abilities must be focused on achieving this result. His art is measured by the degree of his success. He must gauge the public preference, and there is no reliable blueprint for him to follow.

Classical music has generated complete libraries of scholarly opinion and analysis and supports a sizable population of critics whose sole purpose is the interpretation and explanation of musical compositions and performances. There is no such corresponding establishment for popular music, nor is there need for any.

Popular music, by definition, must be popular. It follows then that the more popular a piece of music, the better it must be. It is that simple. Instead of consulting learned critics about his art, the popular-music *aficionado* need only consult the lists—compilations of the popular standings of records in terms of over-all sales.

He knows that though it is possible for a good song to be lost in the commercial shuffle—unfortunately, it happens all the time—it is impossible for a song without some redeeming quality to climb to the top of the lists. A place on the top of the lists is where all popular music aspires to go. This is at once the critical gauge of a song's worth and the measure of its success. Public acceptance is the ultimate judge.

Actually, a similar judgment prevails in all art, though it is not always quite this obvious. In the final analysis, art must appeal to people. This is true of painting, literature, theater, music—of all art. For art cannot exist without an audience.

Wolfgang Amadeus Mozart, for example, wrote some forty-five symphonies in his tragically short lifetime. Of these, three are played regularly as part of the standard symphonic repertoire. Some three or four more are revived occasionally as musical curios. The rest did not measure up to the test of time—people do not listen to them. The same holds true for all the master composers—how many times, for example, have you heard Beethoven's Eighth Symphony, or Tchaikovsky's First? Which brings us to another interesting question: Is a work of art great because it survives, or does it survive because it is great?

On occasion, a work of significant art must wait for its audience—an occurrence much rarer than one might expect. Most great artists enjoyed at least some recognition during their lifetime, and many experienced acclaim. It has, however, happened. Johann Sebastian Bach provides a case in point. Though he was fairly successful during his lifetime, his music was generally neglected until it was rediscovered and vigorously championed by Felix Mendelssohn in the mid-nineteenth century. Even so, it was not until well into the twentieth century that Bach regained his well-deserved popularity.

Today we are in the midst of another musical revival

that is pertinent to the experience of Bach. Baroque music is becoming increasingly popular. Whole orchestras have been organized to exploit this fad—yes, Virginia, there are fads in classical music—and no concert season is complete without at least one baroque-music festival. Scarlatti, Purcell, Telemann, Vivaldi, Buxtehude, and other all but forgotten composers are becoming familiar names.

The baroque composers, incidentally, have much in common with our laborers along Tin Pan Alley. They were considered, by their world at large and probably by themselves as well, to be professionals rather than artists. Indeed, the idea of art in music came in with the romantic era, Beethoven being a moving force in this direction. The earlier composers were strictly commercial in their approach in that they created music whose primary aim was to please their musical public rather than to express their souls' innermost yearnings.

We bring this up only to show that motivation has little effect on the end product when it comes to art. It is possible for the most commercially oriented artist to create significant works just as it is possible for the most idealistic artist to create trash. Communication is the primary concern of art and all other considerations pale before it. Technique, form, content are secondary, the means to an end.

And communication is the sole aim of popular music. It does not aspire to educate, to inspire, to broaden, to uplift—*all it wants to do, baby, is be friends with you!* To this end it offers a broad spectrum of expression with something to appeal to everyone.

For those who follow them, the lists—that foolproof gauge of the state of the popular musical arts—provide a surprising variety of musical fare. Despite the wearisome misconception that all pop music sounds the same and it's all rock-and-roll anyway, the lists can hardly be described as one-sided. Even a casual examination of the offerings that scaled these rarefied heights during the past few years will dispel any such notion.

Included in this select company are such divergent musical offerings as a charming folk song, "Dominique," performed by a Belgian nun; "Suki Yaki," a plaintive ballad recorded by Kyo Sakomoto, a Japanese singing idol, which demonstrated that in music, at least, the twain can meet; the title song from a highly successful Broadway musical, *Hello, Dolly!*, sung by Louis Armstrong, that gravel-voiced old jazz great; a modified version of the big-band sound in "A Taste of Honey," expertly performed by Herb Alpert and the Tijuana Brass; "Eve of Destruction," a powerful anti-war song in an emotion-charged performance by young singer Barry McGuire; an instrumental titled "Cast Your Fate to the Winds," performed by a progressive-jazz trio from San Francisco; "Subterranean Homesick Blues," a song without melody or intelligible words as recorded, hauled onto the lists by the raw talent of its composer and singer, Bob Dylan; an old-fashioned romantic ballad, "I Left My Heart in San Francisco," sung by Tony Bennett in a time-tested style familiar to those of us who are over thirty; "Sounds of Silence," another social-protest song performed by Simon and Garfunkel and written by Paul Simon; and a traditional ballad given a half-wicked reading by that past master of the genre, Frank Sinatra, "Strangers in the Night."

The king of the hill during the past ten years or so, however, has been rock-and-roll. Examples of this genre have made up about 80 per cent of all the records on the lists during this period. This is not surprising. This is the age of the rock, and its driving beat and vigorous musical syntax provide the dominant theme for popular music today. What so many critics considered to be nothing more than a passing fad—a moment of musical madness—has demonstrated its durability. During this period, rock-and-roll has grown and spread throughout the world. This development will be traced in Chapter 6.

"It's one of the freshest American type of things ever originated. I love the beat. I love the songs. I love the way the kids do it," says Dick Jacobs of Decca Records, an early champion of the rock.

Within this idiom there is also a great deal of variety. There is a world of difference, for example, between the Detroit sound as developed by the Four Tops and the California sound as interpreted by the Beach Boys; between the Beatles and the Rolling Stones; between the singing styles of Lesley Gore and Petula Clark. For rock-and-roll is more than a musical idiom. Like jazz before it, the rock is a state of mind, a way of relating to the world. It is a musical reflection of our peculiar moment in time, with as many facets as the times themselves.

Popular music encompasses a broad spectrum of musical expression. It ranges from protest songs with strong social messages to nonsense songs whose sole claim to fame lies in novelty of sound or arrangement; from Broadway show tunes to frenetic rock-and-roll; and all to capture the interest of the public for a brief moment of musically induced forgetfulness.

Popular music has not been recognized as an art form until very recently, and even now it is still denied this status by many. Indeed, it was only about sixty years ago that a world-renowned composer, Anton Dvořák, shocked our home-grown Brahmins when he used native American music and themes in a "serious" symphonic work. Till then, genteel musical America looked down its haughty nose at everything native and original.

Today that outlook has changed for the better. The whole question of popular culture is undergoing serious re-evaluation. Artists are discovering unexpected beauties in such "lowbrow" media as comic strips and billboards. Critics are finding undreamed of profundities in the gaudy, popular movies of the 1930's and 1940's. And in music even the despised country and western idiom is being re-examined by musicologists searching for the roots of popular culture.

Thirty-five years ago John Dewey wrote in *Art as Experience* that "the arts that have most validity for the greatest part of the population are not considered arts at all." Dewey then goes on to list them: *comic strips, jazz music, movies, and advertisements.*

Today, we are beginning to appreciate the validity of Dewey's view. Popular music is recognized as an integral part of national culture. As an art form, it occupies a special niche in our lives. We do not come here for heaven-storming revelation nor to hear a message for the ages. Popular music gives expression to the small joys and sorrows that our lives, for the most part, are made of. An art that reflects the moment, it is as permanent as a rainbow and as substantial as a cloud.

2 BIG BUSINESS

Mary had a little lamb,
Its fleece was white as snow,
And everywhere that Mary went
Her lamb was sure to go.

When these words—scratchy, distorted, barely audible—
were reproduced by Thomas Alva Edison in August 1877
on a primitive mechanical device, they ushered in a revolution in popular music whose effects are felt to this day.
To appreciate the extent of this influence, we need only
compare the state of the popular musical arts then and
now. The differences, as we shall see, were largely determined by the effects of Edison's brain child.

The most obvious change can be described simply. At
the turn of the century (when the manufacture of records
and phonographs began in earnest) popular music was

written primarily for singing. Today, it is composed to be performed. In that distant day singing was a community activity. Today, it is more in line with spectator sports. In the 1890's, sheet-music sales were the mainstay of the industry. Now, it is record sales. Then, people said, "Everybody's singing it." Today, we say, "Everybody's listening."

This fundamental change can be seen clearly when we compare songs from then and now. "A Bicycle Built for Two," or "Daisy Bell," written by Harry Dacre in 1892, is typical of the "singing" songs that have come down to us from the Gay Nineties. It remains a favorite. People still sing about Daisy and her not very stylish marriage. An appealing melody, well within the range of an untrained voice; simple, sunny lyrics that are easy to memorize; and a musical structure that lends itself to uncomplicated harmony. These are the characteristics of the popular songs from the era before the phonograph.

These were songs that an amateur barbershop quartet would be comfortable with. Families could gather around the parlor piano to sing them on a Sunday afternoon. Untroubled, sentimental, a bit naïve, they offer a glimpse of an era that has disappeared forever.

Compare this to a contemporary song. A good example might be "Leader of the Pack," as performed by a very popular female vocal group with the unlikely name of the Shangri-Las. This was one of their big hits and commanded a place high on the lists throughout the summer of 1965. The recording which captured the fancy of the record-buying public for this brief span of time is the result of a complex production.

The song itself was composed specifically for the Shangri-Las. The lyrics, melody, orchestration, and arrangement were designed to enhance and focus on a quality of sound and style developed by the group. Included in the end product as represented by the finished record are the sounds of a motorcycle engine, the squeal of brakes, talk, electronic distortion of the singing voices, over-dubbing of various instrumental sounds, and an orchestra consisting of electric guitars, drums, bass, electric organ, brass, woodwinds, and strings.

As an expression, "Leader of the Pack" is related to collage as it developed in the visual arts. In collage, artists utilize real objects—anything from a scrap of newspaper to a full-size mattress—which are incorporated in their compositions. By so doing, the artist attempts to make his work more tactile, more immediately related to the experience of the viewer. Real objects, used in this manner, provide an added dimension to the creation of the artist.

The real sounds used in "Leader of the Pack"—motorcycle engine, squeal of brakes, talk—provide a similar effect. They involve the listener more fully in the performance. Just as real objects are integrated into the composition of a painting, so are these real sounds integrated into the musical structure of this record.

As a song, "Leader of the Pack" would be all but impossible to sing casually on a street corner. Nor was it meant to be. It is an electronic expression projected on the medium of the recording tape, depending as much on electronic techniques for its ultimate effect as it does on the voice and the sounds of the instruments used in the orchestration. It exploits electronic sound potential just as the symphony orchestra exploits the tonal potential of different instrumental groups played in combination.

Indeed, the development of the symphony orchestra can also be traced to technological advances, in this case the manufacture of tempered wind instruments which were perfected in the mid-eighteenth century. This technical development made it possible for large choirs of brass and woodwinds to play along with strings in something approaching reasonable intonation.

The strings, which bridged the period from the baroque, with its small, intimate ensembles, to the romantic and the huge symphony orchestra, also had to be modified to enable the string sound to hold its own against the newly perfected winds. This was done, in the case of the violin, by lengthening the neck, changing the slope of the strings, reshaping the bridge, and strengthening the bass bar. The bow was also completely redesigned. These modifications produced an instrument with a stronger, more brilliant sound. This sound saved the modern string choir from the fate of the viola d'amore and the quinton, along with a number of other small-toned, sweet-sounding stringed instruments that survive today only as musical curios.

Just as the reshuffling of its component parts brings a new dimension to the sound of the violin, so do electronic recording techniques bring a new dimension to the sound of the voice. The symphony orchestra exploits the sounds of instruments perfected in the eighteenth century. Today's recording techniques exploit the tonal possibilities provided by electronics.

Seen like this, electronic innovations represent a legitimate musical development. It is no more *unnatural* to modify the voice electronically than it is to blow a stream of air across the mouthpiece of the modern flute—a precision-engineered instrument machined to a tolerance measured in thousandths of an inch. Both represent technical advances that can be incorporated into the stream of musical development.

A recent casualty of this changeover from song to performance was a once popular program called *The Hit Parade,* long a staple of both radio and early television. For those of you who do not remember, this was a weekly program, performed by a regular staff, that reviewed current song hits. As long as the "song" was the hit the program remained feasible. When the emphasis shifted to "performance," *The Hit Parade* format lost its impact. A song performed by the Beatles, for example, would not be the same when sung by Snooky Lanson—or anyone else for that matter.

This change, engendered by the record industry, was foreseen by John Philip Sousa, "The March King." When he first heard a phonograph record, he realized its implications and is reported to have remarked: "With the phonograph, vocal exercise will go out of vogue. Then what of the national throat? Will it not weaken? What of the national chest? Will it not shrink?"

Oddly enough, the originators of the phonograph did not envision its musical influence. The phonograph was developed in relation to the telephone and telegraph and was conceived of originally as a business aid. It was meant to provide a permanent, accurate, and easily obtained record of telephone conversations and business conferences. This function of the device was reflected in the names given it by the earliest inventors and developers: phonograph, gramophone, graphaphone, phono autograph, and so forth—all of which implied writing with sound.

In Edison's phonograph, the record was made by pressing indentations into a sheet of tin foil by means of a metal stylus attached to a diaphragm that was set into the throat of a horn. The horn acted as a focus for picking up sound waves that were directed to the diaphragm. The tin foil was wrapped around a cylinder that rotated as the sounds directed into the horn were being recorded. A thread on the shaft which held the cylinder moved the foil axially as it rotated, so that the groove impressed on the foil was helical. That is, the groove was in the form of a single line wrapped round and round the cylindrical tin foil like the thread on a screw.

To reproduce the sound, the groove was rerun under the stylus tip with only enough pressure to maintain contact with the groove. In this way, the recording process was simply reversed. The stylus picked up the indentations in the tin foil and transferred them to the diaphragm, activating this member to produce sound waves corresponding to those embossed on the surface of the tin foil. The sound waves were then channeled out of the horn and into the surrounding air.

Although Edison took steps to exploit his invention, he was diverted to the development of the incandescent lamp and electric power systems. He abandoned the phonograph and did not return to its development for some ten years. He did, however, license the Edison Speaking Phonograph Company to manufacture and exhibit the device. For the next decade the phonograph remained nothing more than a novelty exhibition.

While Edison's "speaking phonograph" toured the theatrical circuits, its inventor too busy for the time being to devote himself to its improvement, other inventors became involved with this fascinating gadget. Prominent among these was Alexander Graham Bell, inventor of the telephone. Working with two associates, his cousin Chichester Bell and Sumner Tainter, at Bell's Volta Laboratory in Washington, D.C., Alexander Bell developed an improved version called the graphaphone.

Although similar in appearance and function to Edison's model, the new Bell device had two significant improvements. First, instead of using a tin-foil cylinder, it embossed a groove in wax. Wax, being softer than tin foil, offered less resistance to the engraving stylus, thereby allowing for a more accurately defined groove. This change resulted in a significant gain in both the definition and the volume of the sound reproduced.

The second improvement involved the stylus. The Edison model used the same stylus for recording and reproducing sound. The Bell model used two styluses—one for recording and another, loosely mounted, for reproducing the sound. This "free-floating" needle could be more easily guided along the groove in the wax cylinder and was far superior in sound production. The Volta Laboratory obtained a patent for the device on May 4, 1886.

During this same period, German-born Emile Berliner, another inventor, also turned his attention to sound recording. In his experiments, Berliner took a completely new approach. The initial step in his recording operation was the tracing of a groove as a spiral on a flat disk rather than a helix on a cylinder. Berliner's disk was made of zinc coated with an acid-resistant layer of a fatty substance. The recording stylus etched a groove in the coating, exposing the zinc where the scribe had left its line. An acid bath then left a groove in the zinc disk whose depth could be controlled by the duration and strength of the acid treatment.

Another significant difference in the Berliner process lay in the fact that the vibrations were recorded as sidewise deflections in a groove of uniform depth rather than as variations in the depth of the groove as occurred in both the Edison and Bell processes. In this way, Berliner obtained a record that could be played by means of an appropriately designed reproducing mechanism. His zinc, acid-etched record, however, was not meant to be played. Instead, a negative was made from the master by electroforming, and this negative was used as a mold from which any number of records could be manufactured out of a suitable thermoplastic material.

Berliner used a number of materials to mold his records, including vulcanite and hard rubber, none of which proved satisfactory. Finally, he found a company that could mold the records from a mixture of shellac and wax, which later became standard for all records. The resulting record was superior to both the wax and tin-foil cylinders of his predecessors in many respects. It was harder and more durable, and because the master was cut in a soft, fatty substance there was less cutting resistance and a larger and clearer sound could be reproduced.

Both the Edison and Bell inventions were basically home recording machines. That is, you could make your own record and play it back over the same mechanism. In the Berliner development, the recording and reproducing functions were separated. One mechanism made the master; another played the records back.

Small-scale manufacture of the gramophone, as Berliner

called his reproducing machine, began in 1894. The gramophone was simpler than the cylindrical machines of Edison and Bell and could be sold at a much lower price. One drawback to the promotion of the gramophone was that it could not play back the buyer's voice. Records, however, could be manufactured easily and inexpensively through Berliner's process, and the obvious superiority of the sound produced tended to overcome initial sales resistance.

More serious was the question of a power supply for the machine. The Bell device was driven by a battery-powered motor. Although this was satisfactory as far as performance went, the battery was expensive and cumbersome. Edison's and Berliner's first machines were driven by a hand crank, admittedly a poor source of power from the viewpoint of both performance and utility. It was a nuisance to have to stand there and turn the crank, and it was almost impossible to maintain a constant speed.

Berliner recognized the need for a reliable clockwork drive and controlled speed. This problem was eventually solved by Eldridge R. Johnson, a part-time inventor who operated a small machine shop in Camden, New Jersey. Berliner came to him with the problem, and Johnson worked out a practical design for a spring-driven motor with a friction governor. So successful was this drive that Berliner retained Johnson as manufacturer of the Berliner gramophone.

This partnership was to prove fruitful for the budding record industry. Johnson turned out to be an important innovator who added a number of significant patents in both the recording and reproducing aspects of sound reproduction. His clockwork drive, for example, soon became standard and was adapted with minor variations throughout the industry. In addition, Johnson designed a superior "soundbox" whose principal features were retained with little change throughout most of the history of the acoustic phonograph.

In 1901 Johnson and Berliner formed a new company for the manufacture and sale of records and gramophones. It was called the Victor Talking Machine Company. Stock in the new company went to Johnson and Berliner, with the controlling interest in Johnson's hand. By this time there were three major companies competing in the field: Columbia Records, which developed around the Bell patents, the Edison Speaking Machine Company, and the Victor Company. There were a number of smaller companies also manufacturing phonographs, but most of these were marginal operations with little influence on the over-all development of the industry.

The steady improvement of recording technique and sound reproduction brought the industry to the point where the phonograph became important as a source of home entertainment and not merely as an interesting novelty. Commercial recording, which began in the 1890's, experienced a phenomenal growth. Most of these earliest records were of vaudeville skits, leaning heavily on monologues and humorous stories, but there were also a number of musical selections by bands, singers, and whistlers. People all over the country flocked to hear them. Nickelodeons opened in storefronts; people could for a nickel listen to recordings through earphones plugged into a master machine —the forerunner of today's ubiquitous jukebox.

What began as a "telephone repeater" had discovered its true vocation. This development was pragmatic and had not been envisioned by the original inventors. People re-

sponded to the scratchy, raucous sounds of the early phonograph and demanded more. The industry expanded to meet
this demand. The primary function of the phonograph was
not destined to be that of a business aid, though it is used
in this capacity. Entertainment was the role that Edison's
brain child was meant to play.

By the mid-1900's, many first-rank instrumentalists and
singers were to be heard on records and a mad scramble
to record still others had begun. "Celebrity Disks" were
being issued by Columbia, followed soon after by the "Red
Seal" list of Victor. By 1910, practically every singer and
instrumentalist of note was represented on records. Orchestral accompaniment to vocal selections began to be released
in 1906 after an unsuccessful start in 1900.

So great was the popularity of recorded music that the
influence of the industry began to take effect on both musical content and style almost immediately. Many instruments,
for example, did not record well. These were sacrificed to
those that did. Wind instruments recorded better than
most others, and there was a corresponding tendency to
rely on them, especially in dance and popular music of all
kinds. The voice recorded well, but the strings did not.
Orchestras had to be kept small and loud, with the musicians
crowded close around the recording horn.

Certain rhythmic patterns reproduced more readily than
others, and these, too, became emphasized at the expense of
others. The syncopated, highly articulated rhythms of ragtime, for example, were ideally suited to early recording
contingencies. Purely technical considerations of the recording process, then, began in large measure to determine what
sort of musical fare was being recorded. The immense popularity of the phonograph, in turn, guaranteed that this kind

of musical fare would have a broad exposure to the listening public.

One of the earliest casualties was the string orchestra. At the turn of the century, string orchestras—violins, cellos, and violas—provided the basic musical vehicle. Dance halls, cabarets, restaurants, night clubs, all featured string orchestras as part of their entertainment. Within little more than a decade this kind of ensemble all but disappeared, replaced by small bands dominated by wind instruments—trumpet, saxophone, trombone, clarinet—with strings reduced to bass and guitar, both of which were used primarily as rhythm instruments.

It is difficult to determine precisely why this change occurred. Certainly there were a number of factors involved. It cannot be denied, however, that the record industry played a primary role in this conversion, just as it played a primary role in the growing popularity of ragtime and early jazz. This type of music recorded well and was thus made available to the public.

The exposure led directly to what was described as a national mania. Overnight, it seemed, the country had gone dance crazy. This phenomenon was duly noted and discussed in an article in the October 1913 issue of the highly respected magazine *Current Opinion*. The article, "New Reflections on the Dancing Mania," attributed the craze to the rhythms of ragtime and to their wide dissemination by the phonograph. The article went on to say that

> people who have not danced in twenty years have been dancing, during the past summer, afternoons as well as evenings. Up-to-date restaurants provide a dancing floor so that patrons may lose no time while the waiter is changing plates. Cabaret

artists are disappearing except as interludes while people re-
cover their breaths for the following number. One wishes
either to dance or to watch and to criticize those who do dance.

The record companies took prompt advantage of this
country-wide inclination to shuffle about on a dance floor.
Tangos, turkey trots, foxtrots, and bostons came in a flood
from the record presses.

The dance mania propelled the fledgling record industry
into the big time. Early in 1914 the record trade magazine
Talking Machine made a coast-to-coast survey of the effects
of the dance craze on record sales. The reports were uni-
formly extravagant: dance records—any and all kinds—were
the socko-smash of the day. Between 1913 and 1915, Victor's assets leaped from some $13,000,000.00 to more than
$22,000,000.00.

For the next ten years America danced and the record
industry prospered. During this period the acoustical phonograph was steadily improved. Sound became louder, clearer,
while the manufacture of records became more refined. Still,
fidelity was severely limited by the recording process. Sound
itself provided the energy for cutting masters. Bands, singers,
instrumentalists had to play or sing directly into a recording
horn at the top of their levels in order to activate the cutting
stylus. Within these limits, however, records became as
true and accurate as the process permitted.

Ironically, the next great technical advance appeared to
have doomed the phonograph industry when it appeared.
This, of course, was radio. The radio boom began in the
early 1920's, a development of the technical advances that
arose out of research in wireless telegraphy, as radio was

then called, during World War I. Out of this research came the first practical microphones and amplifiers. Capitalizing on these developments, commercial radio broadcasting was started.

At first there was little to hear and the early radio sets were annoyingly given to emitting unearthly whistles and screeches. Still, people listened. One thing was obvious from the start, the radio receiver of the early 1920's, for all the inadequacies of its amplifier and loudspeaker, offered a quality of sound production that even the finest acoustic phonograph could not approach. Suddenly people realized that machine-made music need not sound tinny and muffled and scratchy. The radio may have been woefully inadequate, but what you did hear sounded more like real music than anything the phonograph could produce.

The next step for the record companies should have been obvious: combine the radio with the phonograph. Actually, electrical recording had been a matter of speculation for some time. As early as 1903 a patent had been issued for an electro-mechanical recorder, but without the condenser and vacuum-tube amplifier its potentiality could not be realized. By the early 1920's, however, both components were available and the practical realization of electrical recording was open to anyone who cared to tackle the problem.

Two English experimenters, Lionel Guest and H. O. Merriman, are credited with making the first publicized electrical recording. They began experimenting in 1919, using a home-built laboratory they set up in a London garage. On Armistice Day, 1920, they recorded the burial service for the Unknown Soldier at Westminster Abbey. The sound was relayed from the Abbey to the recording apparatus in a nearby building over a telephone line. Like most first attempts it was rough and only partially successful. However, the sound quality they achieved and, even more important, the ease with which the record was made represented a revolutionary development in the manufacture of records.

In America, the initiative for developing electrical recording techniques was assumed by the Bell Telephone Laboratories, the research division of American Telephone and Telegraph Company. A team of engineers and technicians began experiments in the late fall of 1919 under the general supervision of Joseph P. Maxfield. For the first time, the recording process was subjected to a thorough scientific analysis and discipline. Before this, the phonograph had developed primarily through a process of trial and error. In the process, a large body of empirical knowledge had accumulated, but there was no unifying theory to connect this accumulation of disjointed facts.

Actually, what this development signified was the end of the tinkering, solitary inventor as far as the phonograph was concerned. The Edisons, the Berliners, the Johnsons, for all their native inventiveness and originality, were no longer a match for the problems posed to the record industry. These problems had to be attacked systematically, and only a highly disciplined team bringing together experts from such fields as physics, engineering, and mathematics could do the job.

This is precisely what happened at the Bell Laboratories, where just such a team applied their disciplines to the problems of sound reproduction. Specifications for an electromagnetic recording head were drawn up and translated into tangible equipment. Microphones for picking up the sound were perfected, and the entire problem of the acoustical properties of the recording studio were thoroughly explored.

An improved acoustical phonograph to play electrical recordings was also developed by the team. This derived from mathematical equations developed for telephone transmission which were translated into mechanical equivalents for application to sound transmission in the phonograph. Energy, the Bell engineers reasoned, obeys the same mathematical laws whether it be in mechanical or electrical form. By using a list of corresponding constants, a known electrical equation can be converted to an analogous mechanical equation.

Thus was born on the drawing boards of a team of engineers, mathematicians, and physicists working together to solve a complex problem, the exponential-horn phonograph which became familiar to the world as the orthophonic Victrola.

Looking back now, it seems odd that a mechanical phonograph should have been developed to play the new electrical recordings. Why not develop an electrical player, since the necessary equipment was available at the time and electrical amplification played the central role in the electrical recording process? Actually, it was entirely possible, and Bell Laboratories did build an all-electric phonograph using an electromagnetic pickup, a vacuum tube amplifier, and a loudspeaker. The resulting set, however, was prohibitively expensive to manufacture, and the sound was seriously prone to distortion.

In order to reproduce sound, this equipment had to perform a number of complex functions. First of all, the electric phonograph must transform mechanical energy picked up from the record groove by the stylus into electrical energy. Second, it must amplify this signal and then transform it back into mechanical energy (sound waves) by means of the loudspeaker. The equipment available in 1924 did not do this very efficiently. The Bell engineers decided to concentrate on the cheaper and acoustically purer exponential-horn phonograph as more practical for home use.

This new recording technique, together with the exponential-horn phonograph, resulted in three radical improvements in the reproduction of sound. First, the frequency range was extended by two and a half octaves so that it now could generate a range encompassing 100 to 5,000 cycles. Bass frequencies never before heard on a phonograph record added body and weight to music, while the newly added treble frequencies introduced a definition and detail previously impossible to produce. Second, the "atmosphere" surrounding a live musical performance could now be partially simulated on records. For the first time musicians and performers were not forced to work in cramped quarters at the top of their sound levels in front of the recording horn. Now they could work in spacious studios with all the proper reverberation characteristics. The electrically amplified microphone system did not depend on sheer force of sound to activate the cutting stylus, as had the old mechanical system. Third, records were louder, clearer, with less surface noise and blast.

The introduction of electrical recording in the mid-1920's marked the beginning of the second period in the development of the phonograph. Sound quality had been greatly enhanced, and this factor, coupled with the new ease of recording with the electric microphone pickup, encouraged the production of more ambitious musical sound. Orchestras became larger, and dance tunes were enriched with an almost symphonic depth of sound. The buying public responded to these developments enthusiastically and the industry thrived. In 1927, 107,000,000 records were sold along with 1,000,000 phonographs.

This happy state of affairs, however, was destined to be short lived. For one thing, progress in electronics, which did so much to improve the quality of records, was also having its effect on radio broadcasting. During this period the radio networks were also enjoying a boom, and this boom was in direct competition with the record companies. The most significant factor, however, was the financial crisis that rocked the world after the stock-market collapse of 1929. The effects of this calamity all but destroyed the record industry.

By 1932, three years after the crash, record sales had dwindled to a grand total of 6,000,000. Columbia Records went into bankruptcy. Victor Records had become a subsidiary of the Radio Corporation of America and its huge Camden, New Jersey, plant had been turned almost exclusively into a facility for manufacturing radios. The victrola in the parlor, which had seemed to be a universal fixture in America, passed from the scene. There was little evidence to suggest that it would ever come back.

What had happened? Why had record sales fallen from 107,000,000 in 1927 to 6,000,000 in 1932? Part of the reason could be attributed to the Great Depression. All business suffered, but not to this disastrous extent. The principal culprit in this drama was undoubtedly radio. Entertainment on the air had reached professional caliber and it was free— a potent attraction at a time when jobs were scarce and wages were low. All the music you wanted to hear was there with the turning of a dial. Why spend money on the new dance record when it was being played twenty-four hours a day?

As far as the record industry was concerned, things could not have been worse, and indeed 1932 proved to be the low point for the industry. Then a new administration in Washington managed to inject a stimulant into the badly shaken economy, and the reaction reached even the sorely pressed phonograph industry. Record sales began to pick up in 1933. In fact, they doubled, but the sale of 12,000,000 records could hardly be cause for celebration when compared to the figures for the previous decade.

Sales of phonographs fared even more poorly. Since 1930 the manufacture of phonographs had all but stopped. People simply were not buying them. Those that survived were obsolete and, more often than not, were gathering dust in the basement, out of sight and out of mind.

There were, however, upward of 20,000,000 radios in American homes, and most of them could be easily adapted to play records. All that was needed was a suitable hookup and turntable. These sets represented a potentially dazzling market—a market that could not be ignored for long. In September 1934, R.C.A. Victor introduced a simple attachment called the Duo Jr., consisting of an electrically powered turntable and a magnetic pickup mounted in a neat wooden box. When attached to a radio set of adequate size and power, it reproduced records remarkably well.

The Duo Jr. was followed by a number of similar attachments. The principal attraction of these mechanisms was their price, which ranged between $15 and $20. These sets were not only made as inexpensively as possible, but in some cases they were practically given away. Victor, for example, offered its Duo Jr. as a premium with the purchase of a certain number of records. Thousands of people obtained these attachments, and their presence provided a good part of the impetus for overcoming the national resistance to record-buying.

Another potent factor in the recovery of the industry was the growing popularity of swing. People all over the country were doing the lindy hop and the big apple and listening to the big-band arrangements of a stylized form of jazz. Decca Records was organized in 1934 by Jack Kapp and E. R. Lewis to exploit this popularity. Based on a policy of providing a quality record at a moderate cost—thirty-five cents at that time—the new company prospered. Such musical personalities and orchestras as Bing Crosby, the Dorsey Brothers, Guy Lombardo, Glen Gray, Fletcher Henderson, the Mills Brothers, and Arthur Tracy were featured in the Decca catalogue. To remain competitive, Victor followed suit with its Bluebird label, which offered name bands in a ten-inch dance record for the same price.

By December 1936 Victor was able to announce a monthly sales total of 1,200,000 records—900,000 of which were popular dance selections. Of this total a good proportion went into a gaudily colored machine that would play your favorite song for a nickel. It was called a jukebox and seemed to be the latest word in musical promotion to the teen-agers, who invested millions of nickels in order to hear

Benny Goodman, the "King of Swing," or to "Swing and Sway with Sammy Kaye."

Actually, the jukebox craze was nothing new. A similar phase had been experienced in the 1890's with wax cylinders and earphones. Coin phonographs of one kind or another had been around for a long time, but like everything else during the depression they had gone into a serious decline. They came out of retirement with the end of Prohibition and were soon established in drugstores, bars, diners, and candy stores. By 1939 there were almost 225,000 of them, and it took 13,000,000 records a year to keep them filled.

For the record industry, the jukebox served two functions. It was both a buyer and a seller of records. Millions of records were sold because they had been heard on a jukebox. With steadily rising sales, it became possible once more to speak of record best-sellers. In 1936 a record of "The Music Goes Round and Round" sold more than 100,000 copies. By 1939 the ceiling had risen to 300,000 with Victor's "Beer Barrel Polka" and Decca's "A-Tisket A-Tasket."

The great record slump seemed to be over. In 1940 record sales soared above the 100,000,000 mark for the first time in more than a decade, and 1941 was an even better year. Under normal circumstances, recovery should have been complete. The times, however, were anything but normal. On December 7, 1941, Pearl Harbor was attacked by Japan and America was at war. Among the first casualties of the war in the Pacific was shellac—the basic ingredient of the phonograph record. In April 1942 the War Production Board ordered a 70 per cent cut in the non-military use of this ingredient. At about the same time the nation's manufacturers of electrical goods turned out their last civilian radios and phonographs. The industry had to dig in for the duration.

Although the industry was more or less dormant during the war, military research in communications and radar was destined to provide a boom in the guise of dramatic technical advances. These developments were exploited, after hostilities ceased, to bring the industry into its third and current phase.

The revolution that marked the beginning of this period came in 1948 with the introduction of the micro-groove long-playing record. This disk could provide thirty minutes of uninterrupted playing time on each side, and the fidelity of sound reproduction reflected the wartime advances in electronic techniques. Surface noise was eliminated, and the acoustic range was extended beyond the limits discernible by the human ear. A record could now be made that would faithfully reproduce all the sounds, overtones, and harmonies generated by even the largest orchestras. The public responded to this development by indulging in an unprecedented buying spree.

A second, equally significant advance was provided by the introduction of a practical magnetic-tape-recording process. In a time of soaring production costs, the advantages of tape-recording were obvious. No longer did soloist and orchestra have to repeat compositions many times in order to achieve an adequate performance. Instead, sections containing flaws could be rerecorded and the section simply spliced into the master.

As a result, recordings achieved a level of performance perfection hitherto deemed impossible. Indeed, there were some critics who maintained that the tape process produced a performance that was too letter-perfect, a performance that, consequently, lacked the realism of a live rendition. But musicians, soloists, singers—and, most important, the public—reacted enthusiastically.

An additional benefit of the tape-recording process was the ease with which a recording could be made. A tape-recording machine could be easily set up in a concert hall, theater, or night club to record actual performances. It also brought the cost of recording down dramatically, providing the possibility for all kinds of record projects that would have been too costly with the old methods. As a result, small, independent recording companies mushroomed. With imagination, enterprise, and very little money, a daring producer could compete with the giants. The variety and scope of musical offerings became staggering, to the great delight and advantage of the record-buying public.

What the long playing record did for symphonies, opera, and Broadway musicals, the seven-inch 45 rpm did for the bread-and-butter staple of the industry—the single popular record. For a time, the industry experienced what is now called "the battle of the speeds," with the 45-rpm record competing with the 33⅓-rpm LP record for a dominant position. By the early 1950's, however, the battle was over and the musical territories had been neatly divided. Pop singles were to be 45's; albums and classical records were LP's.

This armistice came just in time for the industry to capitalize on the next musical development—the phenomenal popularity of a new kind of music called rock-and-roll which propelled record sales to hitherto unimagined totals.

Throughout this historical development, the record industry exerted a profound influence on popular music. Indeed, the state of the recording arts determined to an overwhelming extent the kind of music that was composed, performed, and listened to. During the earliest period of mechanical recording the sound produced was raucous, brisk, and tinny. It was ideally suited to the ragtime rhythms and Dixieland jazz styles that had remained popular through the 1920's. This was the era of the foxtrot and the two-step, of the charleston and the black bottom, and without the scratchy, wheezy phonograph our popular music of the period might have had a different rhythm.

The improvement in sound production through electronic means that occurred in the latter part of the 1920's brought a completely new dimension to recorded music. With this new sound potential came a marked change in the public taste. Within a very short span of time the small Dixieland and ragtime orchestras, generally no larger than seven pieces, gave way to the big band. Dance orchestras that numbered as many as thirty or forty appeared, playing a modified version of Dixieland jazz that was called "Swing." The Dorsey Brothers, Glenn Miller, Sammy Kaye, Glen Gray, and Harry James were among the orchestra leaders who toured the country during the late 1930's and 1940's. They brought a new sound, richer and more sonorous than that of the smaller ensembles that preceded them, heavy on the brass and with a complete saxophone choir, that reflected the harmonic subtleties that could be captured on the new records.

Further development of electronic-sound techniques as a result of research for World War II, saw a third revolution in sound. This time it was the actual incorporation of electric-sound modifications into the finished performance. The equipment itself became an instrument. The eight-track recording system offered the producer a level of control over recorded sound hitherto impossible to achieve. The volume and intensity of sound generated by the individual components of the recording orchestra could be controlled, could be made louder or softer, and even over-dubbed on itself to create sonorities that had never been heard before. The voice could be similarly manipulated. A lead melody, for example, could be recorded and then raised and lowered in pitch without affecting the speed, style, or musical phrasing of the singer. This modified musical line could then be added to the original sound, producing harmonic singing, with the precise ensemble of a single voice.

In the face of these developments, the big band simply faded away. The harmonic subtleties and sonority of their huge orchestrations gave way to subtleties and sonorities of electronic techniques. Recording orchestras began to shrink, until today an eighteen-piece recording orchestra is considered big. The smaller group allows for a more spontaneous performance on the part of individual players and can achieve rhythmic and interpretive subtleties that were out of the reach of the big band.

3 IN THE ORBIT OF BROADWAY

When musicologists discuss the American contribution to the world's musical heritage, most will agree on the significance of two indigenous American forms: jazz and musical comedy. These are generally described as America's primary contribution to musical culture. One evolved organically out of the unique experience of a distinct segment of the American population. The other developed out of an amalgamation of styles and forms that took place in the crucible of the American musical stage. Jazz is akin to folk music in that it developed spontaneously in response to the musical needs and genius of a particular people.

41

Musical comedy is more commercial in that its development was shaped and formed through pragmatic response at the box office. Both elements have provided basic source material for American popular music.

Musical comedy, as we know it today, has drawn on a variety of sources in its development. Its genesis can be traced to such divergent forms as the nineteenth-century minstrel show, English music-hall comedy, burlesque in both its original sense of a satirical variety show and the later, still popular identification as a strip-tease spectacular, the French extravaganza, as well as *opera buffa* and the operetta as it developed on the European lyric stage.

Actually, musical comedy is closely related to comic opera—or light opera, or operetta, as it is also called. The two forms are so closely allied that it is difficult to define a line that separates them. Comic opera, roughly speaking, is closer in structure and style to traditional opera, except that it employs more spoken dialogue and, generally, more fanciful plots.

Musical comedy, as it developed on the American stage, is closer to the idea of a play with music. Ideally, music and story line combine in an integrated creation where both elements enhance the movement of the plot. A good libretto, then, is basic to the success of any musical comedy, though it does not necessarily follow that "the play's the thing." Equally important are an appropriate musical background, good melodies, sparkling lyrics, lavish sets, exciting choreography, and—of course—beautiful girls, preferably in scanty costumes.

In the early history of American musical comedy, beautiful girls and comedians were the principal attractions. Both, for example, were conspicuous in such musical entertainments as the famed Ziegfeld Follies. They are still important, but it is a sign of the maturity in the American musical theater that they are no longer primary. Today, libretto, sets, choreography, and acting are the most important attractions.

Musical comedy also occupies a dominant position in contemporary popular music. Music derived from the theater as well as romantic ballads and topical songs strongly influenced by Broadway styles make up the single largest category of the popular repertoire. This repertoire represents the broad "middle-class" of popular musical expression, providing those enduring songs and ballads that, at worst, are inoffensive and, at best, reveal a true genius for melodic invention. These are the songs we hear on television, in night clubs and in the personal appearances of such popular singing stars as Frank Sinatra, Lena Horne, Andy Williams, Barbra Streisand, Tony Bennett, Jerry Vale, and a host of other entertainers.

This repertoire, in turn, is supported almost wholly on the framework of a thirty-two-bar musical form that provides the structural basis for at least 95 per cent of all show tunes and popular ballads. It is probably the most familiar artistic form ever known and permeates practically all of Western popular music, both folk and commercial.

Musically, the thirty-two-bar form is simple. This simplicity, however, is somewhat deceptive. The musical variations that can occur within this framework are practically limitless. As utilized in our popular repertoire, the form is made up of distinct though harmonically related eight-bar phrases divided into an introduction, verse, and refrain. The verse is generally a repeat of the eight-bar introductory phrase with a variation leading to a modulation in the last bars of the repeat, which carries the music into the refrain.

This structure became codified in the hymns of the Protestant Reformation, which drew on secular folk sources for its music in opposition to the elaborate and highly stylized forms that were current in the Catholic Mass. Since church music provided the major source of musical participation for the great part of the population before the flowering of popular secular entertainment in the eighteenth century, the continued use of the thirty-two-bar form in Protestant church services established this structure as the most familiar vehicle for song. Though originally based on secular sources, the Protestant hymnal, in turn, exerted an influence on subsequent secular music, especially as it pertains to popular expression.

As a musical framework, the thirty-two-bar form has demonstrated a remarkable vitality. It has survived for at least the past four hundred years as the dominant singing form and shows no sign of exhaustion. In its way, it provides the perfect vehicle for song. Thirty-two bars allows enough length for harmonic and melodic interest and variation as well as lyric completion, while still remaining short enough for easy memorization and comfortable listening. What began as a revolt against the highly stylized music of the Catholic Mass has become, through a long and involved evolutionary process, a basic factor in American musical comedy.

The thirty-two-bar form, however, provides only one factor in the over-all structure of musical comedy, which developed through its own evolutionary process. In this history, comic opera came first. The success of European works in this style during the latter part of the nineteenth century inspired American composers to try their hands at the genre. These early attempts at American comic opera were copied frankly, as far as music and style were concerned, from the European masters.

One of the first American composers of comic opera was Willard Spenser (1852–1933), a classically trained musician from Philadelphia. His two-act comic opera, *The Little Tycoon*, opened in Philadelphia on January 4, 1886, and proved to be an immediate hit. It became a national success and was produced thousands of times all over the country by both professional and amateur groups.

A frothy, tuneful excursion, the comedy centered on the efforts of a young New Yorker to win the hand of the daughter of wealthy, socially prominent General Knickerbocker—a familiar turn of plot, variations of which still turn up on our lyric stage. The General, in keeping with American upper-class pretensions of the period, hoped to marry his daughter to an English lord.

Our hero, in order to gain status equal to that of the lord, presents himself to the General as "the great tycoon of Japan" in the climax of the plot. The General, properly impressed, grants his daughter's hand and the bride and chorus break into the title song: "Yes, I'll Be the Little Tycoon." It was all very innocent and naïve—and typical. The plot was ridiculous, but the music was sprightly if not particularly original, and the epic did provide a word—tycoon—that found a niche in our popular vocabulary.

Spurred on by the success of Willard Spenser, other academically trained American composers turned their talents to comic opera. Prominent among these newcomers was

Bostonian Woolson Morse (1858–1897), who contributed
two popular stage spectacles, *Wang* (1891) and *Panjandrum*
(1893). Although fairly successful at the time, their principal contribution to the American lyric theater was in
their locales—Siam for *Wang*, and the Philippine Islands for
Panjandrum—establishing a preference for exotic settings
that continues to this day.

Two other proper Bostonians tried their hands at comic
opera during this same period. One was George Chadwick
(1854–1931), who contributed a burlesque opera called
Tabasco (1894) which ran for eight performances; the
other was Edgar Stillman Kelley (1857–1954) whose operetta *Puritania* did a little better, running for a total of a
hundred performances.

All of these American composers of comic opera had
had a classical training in conservatories here and abroad.
Their attempts at this kind of composition were made in an
offhand manner, sandwiched between "real works"—symphonic and choral compositions. What their experience
demonstrated was that comic opera demanded a discipline
of its own. It required more than a solid musical background.
What it called for was a special feel for popular music
acquired only by specific training and experience.

Among the first American composers to apply himself
specifically and professionally to the composition of comic
opera was Reginald De Koven (1859–1920). Born in Mid-
dletown, Connecticut, De Koven received his musical training in England and France where he studied with such
masters as Genée and Delibes. From the start, De Koven's
goal was the composition of comic opera and all of his
energies were channeled toward this end. He studied and

analyzed the scores and styles of all the great composers in this field.

After completing his studies, he returned to America and settled in Chicago. Here, he turned his attention to composition. His first work, *Begum*, was produced in Chicago in 1887, followed the next year by *Don Quixote*, both of which enjoyed only limited success. These works, however, were in the nature of an apprenticeship, the first practical application of the knowledge and skills he had acquired in his studies.

Then, on June 9, 1890, a third operetta, *Robin Hood*, opened in Chicago. This was a romantic comic opera in three acts, based rather loosely on the exploits of the English folk hero. As performed by a company called the Bostonians, *Robin Hood* was an immediate success and enjoyed a run of more than three thousand performances.

The most important figure in the American musical theater at the time, however, was Victor Herbert (1859–1924), a contemporary of De Koven's. Born in Dublin, Herbert received his musical training, both as cellist and composer, in Germany and Austria. A fine cellist, he became a member of the Johann Strauss Orchestra in Vienna when he was barely sixteen years old and later joined the court orchestra in Stuttgart as cello principal. In Stuttgart, Herbert continued his studies in composition with Max Seifritz.

After marrying the Viennese singer Therese Foster in 1886, Herbert came to America, where he was to remain for the rest of his life. He first joined the orchestra of the Metropolitan Opera House as first cellist, while his wife was engaged as a singer; later he played with the Theodore Thomas Orchestra and the New York Philharmonic.

His early compositions, which already revealed his remarkable melodic gifts, were performed by the Philharmonic Orchestra. Herbert himself was soloist in the première
performances of both his cello concerti. From 1898 to 1904
he was conductor of the Pittsburgh Symphony Orchestra,
which he left when he organized the Victor Herbert Orchestra in New York.

Although Herbert supported himself by playing and
conducting during his early years in America, his primary
musical concern was composition. Always prolific, he wrote
a number of cello concerti, symphonic works, and other
serious music before he discovered his *métier*. Herbert's
first operetta was *Prince Ananias,* produced in 1894. Not
only was it a commercial success, enjoying a Broadway run
of four months, but, more important, it provided the ideal
vehicle for Herbert's melodic genius.

With *Prince Ananias,* Herbert had found the form through
which to express his musicality. He turned to operetta with
a vengeance, composing more than forty works during the
next three decades, many of them considered masterpieces
of light opera. Among the more notable were *The Serenade*
(1897), *The Fortune Teller* (1898), *Babes in Toyland*
(1903), *Mlle. Modiste* (1905), *The Red Mill* (1906),
Naughty Marietta (1910), *Sweethearts* (1913), and *Velvet
Lady* (1919).

It is an impressive legacy and is still very much alive.
Herbert's melodic inventiveness and skillful orchestrations
have assured a place for the best of his works in the standard
repertoire of light opera. They are performed throughout
the world by both amateur and professional groups.

His songs have also become standards that are still performed for their delightful melodic richness. "I'm Falling in Love with Someone"; "Ah, Sweet Mystery of Life"; "Because You're You"; "Stout-Hearted Men"; Kiss Me Again"— these are just a few of Victor Herbert's enduring songs.

Another composer of comic opera who must be mentioned was John Philip Sousa. In the course of his colorful career Sousa composed ten comic operas, the most famous of which was *El Capitan,* first produced on Broadway in 1896. Sousa, born in 1854 in Washington, D.C., is, of course, best known for his marches. His interest in marches derived from his post as conductor of the United States Marine band, a position he held for twelve years, from 1880 to 1892. After leaving the Marines, Sousa organized his own band, which won international renown. He composed over a hundred marches, among them "Semper Fidelis" (1888), "The Washington Post March" (1889), "The High School Cadets" (1890), and—most popular of all—"The Stars and Stripes Forever" (1890).

The three decades spanning the years from 1890 to 1929 might be considered the golden age of light opera in America. These were the years that saw a succession of glittering productions grace the musical stage, establishing a tradition of melody, skillful orchestration, and showmanship.

During this same period, however, another kind of musical fare was also enjoying a moment of popularity, though it was a bit more earthy and vulgar and had little of the glitter and none of the glamor of operetta. This entertainment came under a number of colorful names, including burlesque, minstrel, and variety. What these forms lacked in polish, they made up for in vitality and "lowbrow" appeal. Oddly enough, it was out of a synthesis of these two kinds of musical fare that the peculiarly American musical comedy was to emerge.

In tracing this history, most musicologists begin with the production of a remarkable musical extravaganza, *The Black Crook*, which opened at Niblo's Garden in New York City on September 12, 1866. Although it was looked down on by knowledgeable critics of the time as no more than a mélange of variety acts and legs held together by a mere thread of plot, *The Black Crook* was fabulously successful. It ran for more than twenty-five years, setting a record for longevity if not for artistic quality. People flocked to see it, and the production supported a whole generation of performers.

A success of this dimension could not be ignored for long —and it was not. Among the musical entrepreneurs of the time who took notice was Edward E. Rice. He made theatrical history of a kind with his production of *Evangeline,* for which he wrote the music. *Evangeline,* billed as a "burlesque, musical extravaganza," owed much to both style and content to *The Black Crook,* and like its predecessor was a notable success. It ran for more than four years, which is a respectable run by any standards.

Rice followed this success in the vernacular with the production in 1898 of a ragtime musical called *Clorindy, The Origin of the Cake Walk,* which featured an all-Negro cast. With a musical score by Will Marion Cook and a libretto by Paul Laurence Dunbar, this musical excursion was a succession of acts, songs, dances, comic turns, ballads, burlesques, and dancing girls held together with a thin line of plot. Its success could be attributed, in large measure, to the ragtime rage which was then sweeping the country.

It was, however, the first in a long line of all-Negro musicals and its music derived completely from a native American idiom.

Cook, who wrote the music for *Clorindy*, followed this success with a series of popular musical extravaganzas that featured Negro performers. The most notable of these were *Dahomey* (1902), *Abyssinia* (1906), and *Bandana Land* (1907). Cook, a thoroughly trained composer who had studied at the Oberlin Conservatory in Berlin and with Anton Dvořák in New York, also wrote a number of highly successful songs. His most ambitious work, however, never achieved any lasting fame. This was a three-act opera titled *St. Louis 'Ooman*. It is significant today only because in this work Cook anticipated the use of jazz and blues themes by many later composers.

Another important influence in the development of musical comedy was provided by the works of George M. Cohan (1878–1942). Born into a theatrical family, Cohan spent his whole life on the stage, appearing first as an infant with the family vaudeville act. From this beginning, he went on to perform just about every theatrical function. At one time or another, Cohan was actor, dancer, singer, manager, producer, composer, and playwright.

When Cohan starred in a musical called *Little Johnny Jones* in 1904, he introduced one of his own songs, "Yankee Doodle Boy," which became a prototype for his catchy, flag-waving tunes. In 1906, Cohan produced his first musical, *Forty-five Minutes from Broadway*, which was an immediate success. It was followed almost immediately by *George Washington, Jr.* (1906), which featured the patriotic "It's a Grand Old Flag."

Although conservative critics accused Cohan of being vulgar, cheap, and blatant, he went merrily on his way from one popular success to another. Lasting fame came to Cohan when he composed the song that was to become the most popular hit of World War I, "Over There."

The musicals of George M. Cohan served as a bridge between the two concurrent Broadway styles. He borrowed from the earthy, "lowbrow" appeal of the flag-waving, girl-studded extravaganzas of the music halls. At the same time, he was influenced by the slick, professionally polished comic-opera productions. Admittedly, his shows were brash and gaudy, but if not in the best of taste, they did bring to the stage a native energy and pointed the way toward a national musical theater that could draw on American grass-roots genius and invention.

At this time, it must be remembered, the Broadway stage was dominated by light opera. Victor Herbert, Rudolf Friml, Sigmund Romberg—all of them European-born and -trained—were the leading lights in this theatrical galaxy. Their stage productions were frankly derived from European models and their songs, orchestrations, and musical structure were characterized by this international flavor. Their primary contribution to the American lyric stage was the precedent their productions established for craftsmanship and professionalism. From a technical standpoint their work was superior in all phases of lyric theater.

The work of George M. Cohan, then, represents an early synthesis of the polished professionalism of comic opera and the rude, earthy, flamboyant expression of the music hall. This merger was to become even more complete as a result of the immense popularity of ragtime. As we have already seen, ragtime assumed the dimensions of an international craze. All over the world, people flocked to music halls and dance halls to listen and dance to this novel rhythm.

Such popularity could not be ignored for long. People responded to ragtime, and it did not take long for a full-blown, Broadway musical to appear in answer to this response. On December 8, 1914, just such a production opened in New York. It was called *Watch Your Step* and was promoted as a "syncopated musical show." Featured in the elaborate production were Vernon and Irene Castle, the very popular dancing team, and the music, lyrics, and libretto were the work of a rising young theatrical figure named Irving Berlin.

Berlin, who was born in Russia in 1888, came to America as an infant and grew up on New York's Lower East Side. Musically, Berlin was a pioneer in adapting the rhythms and musical syntax of both ragtime and jazz to popular song. He first gained attention with "Alexander's Ragtime Band," which he wrote in 1911. He followed this with a second big hit in 1912, "Everybody's Doing It." Both of these songs reflected his concern with native musical sources.

This concern was also very much in evidence in *Watch Your Step*. The musical score was derived from ragtime. The production, however, was lavish, thoroughly professional, and successful. It proved that a musical derived from native sources could compete with comic opera on the same level when given an adequate production. It also provided an important impetus to a fledgling career, for Irving Berlin went on from this success to establish himself as a major contributor to popular culture.

This career was interrupted by World War I. Like so many of his countrymen, Berlin found himself in the army. His talents, however, were not permitted to lag. In August 1918, while on special leave from the army, Berlin produced a soldier show called *Yip, Yip, Yaphank,* for which he wrote both music and lyrics. The production featured the hit song, "Oh, How I Hate to Get Up in the Morning."

Twenty-four years later this song was revived in another soldier show for another war. *This Is the Army,* also boasting songs and lyrics by Berlin, with a cast drawn from army ranks, opened on July 4, 1942. Like its predecessor, it was an immediate success and the theme song, "This Is the Army, Mr. Jones," became one of the most popular songs of World War II.

Berlin's most important contributions to musical comedy, most authorities agree, were made with two productions: *Face the Music* (1932) and *As Thousands Cheer* (1933). Both had librettos by Moss Hart and both were highly topical and satiric. Police corruption was the theme of *Face the Music. As Thousands Cheer* directed its shafts at everything from the White House to the Metropolitan Opera. One sketch featured Ethel Waters in a song that included what was to become one of the most famous couplets in popular song, "She started a heat wave by making her seat wave."

In these musicals Berlin broke sharply with traditional comic opera. The songs and dances derived from native sources and were held together by a plot rooted in the contemporary scene. Their commercial success proved that there was an enthusiastic audience for this kind of musical treatment.

After the success of these two shows, Berlin went to Hollywood. He returned to Broadway in 1940 with *Louisiana Purchase.* Like his earlier musicals, this too exploited a topical theme with a political satire aimed at Louisiana's Governor Huey Long. In 1946 Berlin climaxed his career with his popular *Annie Get Your Gun,* starring Ethel Merman in the title role of Annie Oakley. For this musical, Berlin wrote some of his most effective songs including: "Doin' What Comes Naturally," "Show Business," "They Say It's Wonderful," and "You Can't Get a Man with a Gun."

Another important milestone in the development of musical comedy was provided by Jerome Kern's perennially popular *Show Boat,* first produced on December 27, 1927. Oscar Hammerstein II wrote the libretto and lyrics from Edna Ferber's novel of the same name. For this production, Kern wrote some of his finest songs, songs that are still performed regularly. These include "Ol' Man River," "Can't Help Lovin' Dat Man," "Why Do I Love You?," "Bill," and "Only Make Believe."

Show Boat tells the story of Cap'n Andy and his musical troupe aboard the Mississippi River steamer *Cotton Blossom.* The love interest centers on Magnolia, the leading lady, and Gaylord Ravenal, the dashing gambler. In the production there is a perfect integration of story line and music, both of which derive from native experience. This factor is central to the structure of the comedy, musically as well as literally, bringing a line of musical development to a logical climax.

Kern is also credited with the discovery of the American West as a favored locale for musical comedy, in his *Red Petticoat* (1912). Then, in 1917, his *Leave It to Jane* introduced the college campus to the American stage, providing still another setting that was to prove fruitful for musical comedy. *Very Good, Eddie* (1915), established a vogue for the intimate musical revue written especially for a small theater.

Probably the most influential figure in musical comedy, however, was George Gershwin (1898–1937). More so than any other composer, he created that mixture of realism, sharp story line, and integrated musical content that have become characteristic of American musical comedy.

Like so many figures in musical history, Gershwin demonstrated his talents early. He was born in Brooklyn, New York, on September 26, 1898. As a youth, he studied piano with Charles Hambitzer and Ernest Hutcheson and harmony and composition with Edward Elenyi and Rubin Goldmark. By the time he was fourteen Gershwin had composed his first popular song, and before he was twenty had written his first musical comedy. Titled *La, La, Lucille,* it was produced on Broadway in 1919. Although neither a critical nor a commercial success, it revealed the promise of a strikingly original talent.

More important, it brought the young composer to the attention of George White, who commissioned Gershwin to write the music for *George White's Scandals*. For this revue, Gershwin wrote "Swanee," which was sung in the production by Al Jolson. The song became the biggest hit of the year and propelled Gershwin to national prominence.

During the next decade the name of George Gershwin became a fixture on Broadway marquees. He continued to write scores for musical comedy and produced a series of spectacular hits that included *Lady Be Good* (1924),

Tip Toes (1925), *Oh Kay!* (1926), *Funny Face* (1927), and *Girl Crazy* (1930). Then, in collaboration with his brother Ira, who wrote the lyrics, Gershwin turned to satire. *Strike Up the Band* (1930) represented a sharp departure from his earlier work. It was topical, satiric, and concerned itself with contemporary social problems. This was followed by another musical in the same vein, *Of Thee I Sing* (1931), which spoofed an American presidential election and its aftermath in the White House. This production was awarded the first Pulitzer Prize ever bestowed on a musical comedy.

Having thoroughly conquered Broadway, Gershwin was now ready to leave musical comedy. He had already achieved a reputation as a serious composer and his rhapsodies and concerti were performed by symphony orchestras all over the world. When he did return to the lyric theater it was with a much more ambitious project. *Porgy and Bess* (1935) soared beyond the limits of musical comedy and is considered by many to be the finest American opera ever written.

Gershwin's place in music is secure. During his career, cut short by his untimely death in 1937 after an unsuccessful operation for a brain tumor, he contributed a remarkably varied list of composition. These include some of our most popular songs, symphonic works that have been accepted into the standard repertoire of the world, a series of brilliant musical comedies, and his masterpiece, *Porgy and Bess.*

In all of his work Gershwin's concern with American musical roots is evident. His symphonic compositions mark the triumph of the popular spirit in the art music of America. He elevated the peculiarly American genius for popular expression to the highest musical plane, and herein lies his principal contribution and the factor that will assure his continued popularity and renown.

The next great milestone in musical comedy came with the works of Richard Rodgers and his lyricists, Lorenz Hart and Oscar Hammerstein II. Rodgers, the son of a doctor, was born in New York City in 1902 and, like Gershwin, displayed his musical talents early. He is reported to have picked out tunes on the family piano when he was only four years old.

While attending Columbia University, Rodgers met Lorenz Hart, his first librettist. The two collaborated on a series of amateur musical shows, beginning an association that was to be one of the most fruitful in the American theater. Their first commercial success came with the production of *A Connecticut Yankee* (1927). In this musical, based on Mark Twain's novel, both the lyrics and the music combined the archaic with the vernacular in a mixture that captured the public fancy.

During the next fifteen years, Rodgers and Hart produced a string of successful musicals including *Present Arms* (1928), *Jumbo* (1935), *On Your Toes* (1936), which featured the realistic ballet sequence, "Slaughter on Tenth Avenue," *Babes in Arms* (1937), *I Married an Angel* (1938), *Too Many Girls* (1939), *Pal Joey* (1940), which was based on a series of short stories by John O'Hara which appeared in *The New Yorker* magazine, and *By Jupiter* (1942).

Then, in 1943, Lorenz Hart died, ending a partnership that was one of the most productive associations in the history of the lyric theater. During their fifteen-year collaboration, Rodgers and Hart wrote twenty-nine musical shows, nine of which were made into motion pictures, and wrote nearly four hundred songs.

After the death of Hart, Rodgers teamed with Oscar Hammerstein II in a collaboration that was to prove no less memorable than the earlier. The first fruit of this partnership was *Oklahoma!* (1943) which remains a landmark in American musical comedy. An adaptation of a regional folk play, *Green Grow the Lilacs,* by Lynn Riggs, the musical version opened in New Haven with the title *Away We Go.* When the tryout moved to Boston, it became *Oklahoma!*

The production opened in New York at the St. James Theater on March 31, 1943. Public reaction was immediate. The show became a mainstay of Broadway and ran for almost six years, achieving a total of 2,202 performances. Touring companies brought the musical to theaters all over the country.

Oklahoma! contained some of Rodgers and Hammerstein's most endearing songs, including such perennial favorites as "People Will Say We're in Love," "Oh, What a Beautiful Morning," "Oklahoma," "The Surrey with a Fringe on Top." All of these songs have demonstrated their enduring quality and have become a part of the standard popular repertoire.

Good songs alone, however, did not give *Oklahoma!* its appeal and historical importance in America's musical theater. Here was a genuinely American musical comedy, different from anything seen on the stage before. It was fresh and friendly and all of a piece. Story line, music, choreography, settings, songs combined in a perfectly integrated expression that established a precedent for quality on all levels that still exerts an influence on musical comedy.

Following the spectacular success of *Oklahoma!*, Rodgers and Hammerstein continued their partnership with a series of notable stage productions: *Carousel* (1945), *Allegro* (1947), *South Pacific* (1949), *The King and I* (1951), *Me and Juliet* (1953), *Pipe Dream* (1955), *The Flower Drum Song* (1958), and *The Sound of Music* (1959). Oscar Hammerstein died in 1960.

The influence of musical comedy has reached into all aspects of popular music. Its effects are evident in the songs we sing and in the manner in which we sing them. Actually, as we have already seen, this influence is a two-way proposition. Musical comedy has drawn liberally from native musical styles and forms. It has taken these elements, refined and perfected them, and returned them to the mainstream of popular culture, enriched substantially in the process.

The principal credit for this development must go to the talented composers and lyricists who shaped the American musical theater. Their work, however, was projected to the public by equally talented performers, who must share in the final laurels. The Ethel Mermans, Mary Martins, Gwen Verdons, Paul Drakes, and Ray Bolgers gave shape to what was once no more than an idea in a composer's head. To a large extent, their special abilities and talents determined the structural emphasis of a production.

On the periphery of the Broadway orbit was a virtual army of performers, both instrumentalists and singers, who also exerted a strong influence on the developing styles and modes of this broad, middle spectrum of popular music. They performed in night clubs and theaters, in concert appearances and in Hollywood spectaculars. Their performances focused primarily on songs, without the support of story line and theatrical setting. They provided the proving ground for the songs that came out of musical comedy. It was one thing to hear a song that was part of an elaborate theatrical production, but quite another to listen to it on its own.

Among this host of singers one performer must be singled out because of the extent of his influence. In the early 1940's, a young man began to make appearances with the big bands of the time. His name was Frank Sinatra. Thin, gangly, neither strikingly handsome nor the possessor of a magnificent voice, there was little about him to suggest the dramatic turn his career would take. About the most that could be said about him by a friendly critic was that "he had a way with a song."

But Sinatra had something more than just a way with a song. He was also possessed of an original musical intelligence—an intelligence that could focus on a factor almost completely ignored by his predecessors: he made a thorough study of the singer's art. In the process, he made a discovery that has influenced every popular singer, male and female, since that time. He discovered the microphone.

Actually, microphones had been used by singers for at least fifteen years before Sinatra came along. They were, however, used primarily to amplify the voice. Sinatra treated the microphone as an instrument, and like any other fledgling instrumentalist he applied himself to the mastery of the techniques necessary to exploit its potential to the full. He became a virtuoso in its use, and this mastery colored all aspects of his performance.

The result was a new singing sound, with a new approach

to phrasing, dynamics, and the emotional content of a song. In its way, this was a revolutionary discovery that has exerted a permanent influence on popular song. If, today, so many singers sound like Sinatra, it can be attributed to the fact that they are using the same instrument—an instrument that Sinatra created.

4 JAZZ

Unlike musical comedy, which developed in response to the commercial considerations of the lyric stage, jazz developed on its own. It was, first of all, the secular music of the Negro people in America, a people whose remarkable musical contribution will be more fully traced in Chapter 9. Jazz evolved in response to the emotional and spiritual demands of this people. Initially, commercial considerations had little, if any, influence on this development.

The origin of the word itself is lost. According to some authorities, *jazz* is a corruption of the Elizabethan *jass*, a word associated with bawdyhouses. Others suggest that

it might derive from the name of some Negro musician—
Jess or Chas. (a common abbreviation for Charles). The
word may have originated from African dialect or it may
have its roots in the French verb *jaser,* meaning to chatter.
However it came about, the word as used to designate a
certain type of music first appeared when a band from
New Orleans appeared in Chicago in 1915 under the billing
of "Brown's Dixieland Jass Band."

Like so many important musical developments, jazz
represents a synthesis, a coming together of various musical
strains. It is a musical hybrid, exhibiting an almost biological
hybrid vitality. In its development, jazz drew on practically
all the melodic and rhythmic resources of the New World.

In jazz we can distinguish traces of Baptist hymns and
Elizabethan ballads; we hear echoes of Negro spirituals, of
blues and the "field holler." Jazz rhythms contain hints of
the French quadrille along with the syncopated meter of
ragtime; we can recognize traces of the foot-tapping pulse
of the country hoedown and mountain reel of Anglo-Saxon
derivation along with the memory of a complex and sophisticated African percussive expression. All of these elements
were assimilated and transformed in the crucible of the
Negro genius to produce that musical flowering which we
call jazz.

Nor was this flowering a sudden, overnight development.
It took a full century for this synthesis to be completed.
The history of this development can be traced by following
the succession of musical waves that spread from the Negro
community into the society at large. This development
follows a single line that runs through plantation slave
celebrations, the minstrel show, and ragtime.

According to tradition, jazz was spawned in the bawdy-houses and honky-tonks of New Orleans' Storyville, where Negro musicians were featured entertainers. More accurately, however, jazz came into being at the turn of the century in many localities throughout the country. Something very much like jazz was being performed at that time wherever Negro musicians found opportunity to play.

Intimations of jazz were heard in such far-flung centers as St. Louis and Chicago, Charleston and New York, Kansas City and Memphis; for, as Ferdinand "Jelly Roll" Morton, one of the pioneers of jazz, described the situation: "Jazz music is a style, not a composition." It was a style that reflected a people and not a particular city or locale. It was a style that was destined to exert a profound influence on every aspect of popular and "art" music in the twentieth century.

Although jazz was "in the air" at the turn of the century, the focal point of its development was undoubtedly New Orleans. There was good reason for this focus. New Orleans, at the time, had a reputation as a tolerant, fun-loving city in whose exuberant life even a black musician might find a niche. Indeed, the annual Mardi Gras, the colorful processions and numerous parades and celebrations that the city was noted for, put a premium on musicians of all kinds.

After Emancipation many Negroes turned to music as a means of earning their livelihood. The reasons for this choice are not difficult to determine. First of all, many Negroes were already musicians. Indeed, the Negro musician was a regular feature of plantation life. Throughout the South, no plantation worthy of the name was without its coterie of black musicians, who entertained at social affairs.

More important, however, was the fact that music provided one of the few—if not only—areas in which a black man was permitted to excel. There are very few people in the world who do not respond to music, and music is an individual accomplishment. A musician must be able to make music. His individual capability is the sole measure of his stature. Family connections, social status, wealth are no substitute for talent. The musician stands or falls on the strength of his individual performance.

Immediately following the Civil War, then, bands of newly emancipated street musicians appeared throughout the South. They sang, danced, and performed to the accompaniment, for the most part, of banjo, guitar, and bones—the traditional instruments of the Negro musician.

A significant number of these street musicians made their way to New Orleans, where they hoped they might be accepted with less reservation than elsewhere in the South. Here, their musical horizons were expanded. For one thing, New Orleans had been a center for the manufacture of wind instruments for many years. These were plentiful and inexpensive, especially since a large store of left-over Confederate and Union army-band instruments had come onto the market. The price of a serviceable instrument came within the range of practically anyone hungry to make music, and the Negro musician had this appetite.

The availability of these instruments together with the presence of an enthusiastic audience led to the organization of bands. In the decades following the Civil War, the sound of the brass band became ubiquitous in New Orleans. Bands —both black and white—accompanied funerals, religious and secular processions, patriotic parades, weddings, lodge parties, excursions, and carnivals. Bands from New Orleans entertained on the big river boats, plying up and down the Mississippi. Bands were used to advertise bargain sales in stores, to focus attention on political speeches, and to promote athletic contests of all kinds. Fully a dozen Negro bands took part in the mammoth funeral procession for President Garfield in 1881.

We cannot be certain exactly how these bands played during the latter half of the nineteenth century. That is, we do not know to what extent they conformed to conventional standards of performance. We do know, from descriptive accounts of the period, that they did not sound like the traditional military band. We also know that the music of the Negro bands was tremendously popular with all the people of New Orleans, Negro and white. Indeed, white musicians of the time complained bitterly about this preference.

The Negro street bands were made up, for the most part, of musicians who worked at other trades and played only in their spare time. They also learned their instruments without benefit of formal training. They learned, instead, through a continual process of experimentation. In this way, a new technique of performance evolved, full of unorthodox sounds and timbres that were never taught in conventional study.

Very few of these musicians, for example, could read music. They were compelled to play by ear rather than by eye. This proved to be a liberating influence. They took familiar popular songs and tunes and transformed them through the unrestricted play of their musical imagination and intelligence.

Gradually, through this kind of spontaneous improvisation, a new style of performance evolved. Guided only by intuition and the emotional impact of the moment, these musicians brought to their music new tonal combinations, never-before-heard dissonances, novel figures of melody, disjointed counterpoints. They also brought the peculiar qualities and devices of Negro singing techniques to this music. In their playing, for example, they emulated the harsh guttural, throaty sounds they used in singing. In so doing, they created a new kind of instrumental tone which has been incorporated into the over-all technique of the winds as a particular sound identified as "dirty."

When these newly evolved instrumental techniques were combined with the syncopated ragtime rhythms, jazz came into being. Blatant, abandoned, vulgar, full of driving energy and imaginative, often outrageous, invention, this was a music calculated to shock the sensibilities of a genteel America. In New Orleans, however, it flourished. This was the music demanded by the clientele of such pleasure domes as The Tuxedo Dance Hall, LuLu White's Mahogany Hall, The 101 Ranch, and Pete LaLa's Café.

Haunts such as these, along Basin Street in the Storyville section of New Orleans, provided the Negro musician with opportunities for employment no other city or district could match at the time. The musician was not extravagantly paid for his services, and even the best of them had to double during the day as barbers, waiters, and laborers. They were, however, encouraged and, at times, idolized. In Storyville, the Negro musician was given the stimulation and acceptance necessary to develop his highly personal style and technique. In Storyville, the jazz musician was king. It is not surprising, then, that New Orleans attracted and developed so many superb musicians.

An interesting parallel may be drawn between New Orleans and jazz, and violin playing and Odessa—also a port at the mouth of an important river, but in the Ukraine, half a world away from Storyville. Just as musicians from New Orleans dominated jazz, so did Odessa's violinists dominate their field, and for similar reasons. In Odessa, a despised minority group, severely circumscribed in their professional opportunities, turned to music—the violin, in this case, probably because it was familiar and inexpensive.

A steady stream of violinists came out of the Moldavanka ghetto, beginning in the first decade of this century, among them such stellar artists as Jascha Heifetz, Mischa Elman, Efrem Zimbalist, Nathan Milstein, David Oistrakh, plus a legion of lesser-known but still excellent violinists. Indeed, during the first half of this century every major symphony orchestra in the world boasted a contingent of Odessa violinists.

In New Orleans, Negroes turned to jazz; in Odessa, Jews turned to the violin. In both cases, the remarkable musical results came about through the channeling of energies that had no other satisfactory outlet. In both cases, music, with its emphasis on individual ability, provided an area in which a member of an oppressed minority group might excel.

One of the first names associated with classic New Orleans jazz is that of Charles "Buddy" Bolden. Tall, slender, strikingly handsome and enterprising, Bolden was a barber with his own shop and the publisher of a popular scandal sheet called *The Cricket*. He learned to play the cornet by himself and organized a band early in the 1890's. Bolden quickly demonstrated his musical abilities both as an instrumentalist and as a conductor and organizer. His inventiveness and originality won him immediate acclaim, and the Bolden band soon was in great demand for parades and dances.

For fifteen years the Bolden band provided a focal point for the development of jazz. Most of the great pioneers of jazz played in this band at one time or another. So great was Bolden's reputation that for years afterward jazz musicians boasted of their association with him. According to Louis Armstrong, Bolden was "a one-man genius—way ahead of them all." It was said that on a quiet day, you could hear the sound of his cornet for miles, while his ability to improvise and embroider a melody with all kinds of exuberant ornaments was an unforgettable aural experience.

Bolden continued to be a dominant influence in New Orleans jazz right up to the time of his breakdown. While playing the cornet in a street-band parade in 1909, Bolden suffered a nervous collapse. He had to be confined to a sanitarium, where he remained until his death in 1931. Bolden left a significant legacy. More so than any other musician, he gave a form to the shapeless mélange of musical styles and syntax that grew out of the experience of the Negro ghetto.

After the loss of Bolden, Freddie Keppard (1883–1932) became the dominant figure in New Orleans jazz. An outstanding cornet player himself, Keppard organized the Olympia Band in 1909, which reigned supreme until the close of Storyville in 1917. Included in this band, which like most classic jazz ensembles was small, consisting of

from five to seven pieces, were such outstanding instrumentalists as Louis "Big-Eye" Nelson (clarinet), Sidney
Bechet (clarinet), Willy Santiago (guitar), Zue Robertson
(trombone), and "King" Oliver (cornet).

Of course, many other bands were active in New Orleans
during this period and they share in the credit for the
development of jazz. It was a bustling time in which the
city seemed to be bursting with creative energy. Competition between bands was intense, as it was among individual
musicians. Bands, as we have already seen, played all over
the city for practically every public affair. Occasionally,
two or more bands—each with its own contingent of admirers—would cross in the street, leading to a kind of musical
free-for-all in which the bands would try to outdo each
other in sheer volume of sound as well as in the variety of
their improvisation.

These bands used whatever songs and melodies were
currently popular as the springboards of their invention.
All music was grist for the jazz mill—patriotic songs, bawdy-
house ballads, music-hall tunes, religious hymns, blues,
French and Spanish dances, minstrel songs, marches—everything and anything was utilized in this musical stew. This
cauldron-like quality of early jazz was described, years later,
by "Jelly Roll" Morton:

> The Tiger Rag I transformed from an old French quadrille,
> which was originally in a lot of different tempos. First, there
> was the introduction—"everybody get your partners!"—and the
> people would go rushing around the hall getting their partners.
> . . . The next strain would be a waltz. . . . Then another strain
> which comes right besides the waltz strain in mazooka time.
> . . . We had two other strains in two-four time. I transformed

these into the Tiger Rag which I also named from the way I
made the "Tiger" roar with my elbow! . . . In one of my earliest
tunes, "New Orleans Blues," you can notice the Spanish tinge.
. . . In fact, if you can't manage to put tinges of Spanish in
your tunes, you will never be able to get the right seasoning,
I call it, for jazz. . . .

During the first decade of this century, then, the pattern
of jazz was established. Primarily a combination of ragtime
rhythm and melodic treatment of the blues, plus a liberal
admixture of a variety of different musical strains, jazz
evolved a musical syntax of its own.

The typical orchestration, for example, derived from blues
singing. There is an early recording, dating back to 1911
or 1912, that demonstrates this derivation. It is a recording
of a blues song called "When a 'Gator Hollers," sung by
Margaret Johnson and accompanied by clarinet, cornet,
and piano. Although the instrumentalists are not listed, the
cornet player may be "King" Oliver.

It is a typical blues song from that period. Margaret
Johnson carries the melodic lead, while the two melody
instruments play discreetly under her voice. The piano is
used as a rhythm instrument, providing the steady beat
that underlies the performance. In the "breaks" between
voice verses, the cornet comes up with its own strident
solos—configurations embroidered around the voice melody.
Occasionally the two instruments join in these bridges in
discordant duets with the clarinet answering the cornet
lead with a real "dirty" intonation.

Singer, cornet, and clarinet together provide a three-part
harmony utilized in a call-and-response pattern that is still
fundamental to the music of West Africa. Take the singer

away, add a trombone, and you still have the three "voices" that sing and answer the melody over a throbbing rhythm. By substituting instruments for voices, the jazz musician created an abstract pattern of sound rooted in a tradition that could be traced to an all but forgotten African heritage.

Cornet, or trumpet, clarinet, and trombone were the instruments chosen by the early jazzmen as the most expressive and flexible, ideally suited to carry the melodic line over the steady pulse of the rhythm. The trumpet generally took the place of the solo or lead singer. It became the leader, sounding the calls to which the other instruments responded. Clarinet (high voice) and trombone (low voice) completed the three-part harmony. Their voices embroider around the lead melody and take their own melodic breaks in turn.

The rhythm section came to consist generally of guitar, bass, and drums. Some of the early bands included banjo and piano along with an occasional tuba to round out the rhythm. The piano, though it was originally treated as a rhythm instrument, came to play a dual role, the melodic capability of the right hand bringing this instrument into association with the melody section.

The next great impetus to the development of jazz came through an unlikely set of circumstances. In 1917 America entered World War I and New Orleans became the site of a large naval base and training center. Storyville, as we have already seen, was notorious. The section was named after the alderman who sponsored the ordinance that reserved this area for organized vice. Since 1887, when it was established, Storyville had flourished.

This period coincided with the rise of jazz. The reasons

were simple. The pleasure palaces of Storyville offered Negro musicians work and, more important, the opportunity to develop their music in response to an accepting, even enthusiastic audience. The government, however, felt that Storyville would provide too much temptation to Navy personnel. As a result of pressure from the Navy and War Departments, New Orleans closed the district in 1917.

Deprived of their livelihoods by the demise of Storyville, musicians began to leave New Orleans. They streamed north to the cabarets and night clubs of Chicago and St. Louis, Memphis and New York, Kansas City and San Francisco. Most of them were welcomed enthusiastically; America had got a taste of jazz through the efforts of touring bands, notably those organized by Joseph "King" Oliver and Freddie Keppard, and demanded more.

"King" Oliver, for example, settled in Chicago in 1918. Here he organized his famous Creole Jazz Band, whose personnel included Jimmy Noone (clarinet), Honoré Dutrey (trombone), Ed Garland (bass), Lillian Hardin (piano), and Minor "Ram" Hall (drums). In 1922 Oliver added a second cornet to the band: a young player from New Orleans named Louis Armstrong.

It was this band, which included some of the greatest early jazz players, that made the recordings in the first half of the 1920's which provide the definitive sound of classic New Orleans jazz. Such masterpieces as "Dippermouth Blues," "High Society," "Mandy Lee," "Canal Street Blues," and "Snake Rag" reveal the rhythmic and melodic flexibility that was at the heart of the style.

In these recordings, despite the limitations imposed by then current recording techniques, the phrasing, the timing, the uncanny ensemble between the two sections of the band achieve a level of musical and instrumental excellence that brought a new dimension to the performance of popular music. The playing is spontaneous, relaxed, and perfectly controlled, demonstrating the freedom and flexibility of this home-grown musical form.

This period also witnessed a further development of the original New Orleans jazz style. In its earliest ragtime and blues derived form, the rhythmic base was built on a whole-note pulse. During the first decade of this century, a half-note beat with syncopation gradually evolved as the preferred jazz meter. Between 1910 and 1930 this was gradually broken up, occasionally with a tango-like syncopation, until by the late 1920's Louis Armstrong had made a quarter-note idea of rhythm irrevocable.

Another important development that occurred during the latter half of the 1920's created a crisis in the further development of jazz. This was the birth of the "big band," with its huge roster of musicians and its carefully worked out arrangements. Probably the first band of this type was organized by Fletcher Henderson, a Negro pianist and arranger from Georgia, who was an influential leader in New York. In 1919, Henderson formed a large orchestra which played at the Roseland dance hall. Among the musicians who played with Henderson at one time or another were Louis Armstrong and Coleman Hawkins, tenor saxophone.

Henderson's band included anywhere from fifteen to twenty-five pieces. Size alone precluded the possibility of extensive improvising on the part of individual musicians. Improvisation had been at the heart of jazz up to this time, but groups of more than nine players could not achieve

the spontaneous cohesion and the smooth ensemble necessary for a true jazz performance. The big band demanded
orchestral arrangements written out in advance that were
carefully rehearsed before the performance. With Fletcher
Henderson the art of the arranger came to assume an increasingly important role in a new phase of jazz music.

Henderson's big band was an immediate success. The
public responded to the rich sonorities and driving rhythms
generated by this kind of ensemble. Roseland became a focal
point for the new jazz, and the crowds that assembled at this
New York dance hall inspired an avalanche of imitators.

Another influence in this development was Edward
"Duke" Ellington. Born in Washington, D.C., in 1899, Ellington studied music at the Pratt Institute of that city and
formed his first band, a small one, in 1918. Although this
band played in the early New Orleans jazz style of the period, Ellington had definite ideas of his own, and these did
not include individual improvisation. From the beginning,
he endeavored to create a personal style, an individual expression in the tradition of "art" composers.

A talented composer and arranger, Ellington quickly rose
to national and international fame, touring Europe with
immense success in 1933. His compositions are marked by
originality, sophistication, and rhythmic smoothness and
include what many musicologists consider masterpieces of
jazz-inspired orchestral works. Constant Lambert, the English musicologist and conductor, described him as "the first
jazz composer of distinction."

The works of Henderson and Ellington pointed the way.
By the end of the 1920's and the early 1930's the big band
dominated jazz. What happened was that large dance

bands were commercially successful, while the small hot-jazz groups were not. This development culminated in the overblown, slick ensembles organized and exploited by Paul Whiteman in the early 1930's. This new sound was called "swing," and it swept the nation.

Jazz, in the New Orleans tradition of spontaneous impro-visation, had practically disappeared in the face of the slick competition. Eddie Condon, the noted jazz guitarist, summed up the situation: "Just about the only place we could play was in our own rooms, at our own request."

A generation of musicians grew up in the 1930's chafing at the bit imposed by the big-band concept of swing. For brilliant, beautiful, and slick though the big band was, it was also completely removed from the original feeling of jazz. The inspired performer had little opportunity to show his mettle. Lost in the orchestrations of the big band, the jazz musician who sought personal expression had to settle for informal "jam" sessions held in the privacy of the dress-ing room between shows.

By the mid-1940's there occurred an instrumental revolt. The result was a resurgence of the small groups, which re-turned to the improvisational tradition of early New Orleans jazz—with one big difference. The musicians who spear-headed this renaissance were more capable, in every aspect of musicianship and instrumental competence, than their untutored predecessors. All of them, for example, were musically literate. They possessed a theoretical background in music, plus a solid instrumental foundation. These were basic requirements during the era of the big band.

They brought this musical sophistication to improvisa-tional jazz with startling results. Spearheaded by the likes

of Charlie Parker, Thelonious Monk, Dizzy Gillespie, John
Lewis, Bud Powell, Max Roach, their music exploded into
an astonishingly brilliant glissando of abstract sound.

This development marked a turning point for jazz. Up
to this time, jazz, in all of its phases, was primarily dance
music. It was performed to be danced to rather than merely
listened to. Its basic function was to involve the audience
in active physical participation. As such, its development
was severely limited by the demands of the dance floor.

What happened during the 1940's was that jazz—improvisational jazz performed by a small, intimate group—
became liberated from the dance floor. It became music
for listening. The inventive brilliance of Charlie Parker
was a prime mover in this direction. Parker had original
ideas about rhythm, melody, and phrase length, together
with a sweeping melodic and harmonic imagination in
improvisation.

Under Parker's direction the rhythm section provided a
new function in the expression of the ensemble. It dis-
pensed with the pulse and took the drummer's foot off
the bass pedal, allowing the rhythm section the freedom
necessary to accent the new rhythms·that the soloists were
generating. The new sound was called "Bop"—after a rhythmical device—and it found an enthusiastic audience.

This new jazz language was formalized and further refined during the 1950's. Jazz became "cool," as epitomized
in a group of orchestral recordings made by trumpeter Miles
Davis with a medium-sized group. This phase was marked
by rhythmic freedom and a sophisticated harmonic development. One of the members of Davis' group was John Lewis,
who later organized the Modern Jazz Quartet which adapted

and assimilated aspects of classical counterpoint and harmonic development in jazz improvisation.

Another pioneer during this period was Thelonious Monk, whose unique compositions for small groups such as "Four in One" and "Criss Cross" introduced the idea of thematically developed improvisation as a form within the jazz tradition. Exploiting this basic idea, tenor saxophonist Theodore "Sonny" Rollins became one of the first horn players in jazz to perform an extended improvisation with thematic development and cohesion.

This line was developed further by the bassist Charlie Mingus, who combined composition and improvisation in a manner suggesting the earliest jazz styles. Ornette Coleman has probably carried the "cool" style of jazz to its most extreme development to date. Coleman's most important innovations are rhythmic and affect the entire ensemble playing. In his groups, for example, drummer and bass may play entirely different rhythms at the same time, against a rhythmic pattern generated by the solo instruments out of the phrasing of their improvised melodic line.

Intonation, in the Coleman style, is also free with the traditional blues note and vocalized inflections elevated to a point where they encompass whole melodic phrases and lines. Improvisation, for the first time, is based on a general thematic outline rather than on the harmonic progression of a theme melody. This style represents a triumph of improvisation over all other aspects of the musical structure of jazz.

What began as the "bottom-waving, vulgar, barbaric howl of the native" has been transformed into a sophisticated, even esoteric expression. It has moved from the saloon to the concert hall, bringing—in the process—improvisation back to the concert hall, where it had all but disappeared since the baroque period.

This development has taken place within a span of no more than fifty years. During all of this time, jazz has exerted a continuous influence on all aspects of popular music. Its beat, its swing, its earthiness have provided the base on which the structure of American popular music rests. Although jazz today hardly qualifies as "popular" music—it is too highly evolved and sophisticated to be placed in this category—it has left its mark and its sound.

The Beatles (left to right), Paul McCartney, George Harrison, John Lennon, and Ringo Starr, warm up at a Shea Stadium concert. The inventiveness of this group has extended the limits of popular music in all of its aspects. (*United Press International*)

Fletcher Henderson, right, confers with Benny Goodman. Henderson was one of the originators of the "Big Band" sound that dominated popular music in the late 1930's and 1940's. (*Wide World*)

Charlie "Bird"
Parker exerted a
pivotal influence on
the development of
modern "cool" jazz.
(*United Press
International*)

Jazzman Duke Ellington's elegant and sophisticated compositions brought jazz to a new level of artistic accomplishment. (*Wide World*)

The Supremes (left to right), Florence Ballard, Mary Wilson, and Diana Ross, brought a rhythm-and-blues singing style to international popularity. (*United Press International*)

Louis "Satchmo" Armstrong provides a living bridge between the earliest periods of jazz to the present. A germinal influence in Dixieland Jazz during the 1920's, Armstrong still exerts a marked influence on both singing and instrumental styles in popular sound. (*United Press International*)

Bert Keyes is an arranger-musician who specializes in rock-and-roll and jazz. (*Photo by Raymond Ross*)

Strings "dig in" during a record session. Seated in the front row (left to right) are Tascha Samaroff, George Ockner, and David Nadien. (*Columbia Records*)

Art Garfunkel (left) and Paul Simon sing out during a studio recording session. (*Columbia Records*)

Peter Matz, right, arranger, relaxes with Barbra Streisand
and crew during rehearsal for the "Color Me Barbra" television special. (*Columbia Records*)

Producer Mike Berniker (foreground) and recording engineer Frank Laico listen intently in the control booth during recording session. (*Columbia Records*)

(Left to right) Singer Jerry Vale, arranger Marty Manning, and producer Ernie Altschuler discuss a change in the arrangement between takes. (*Columbia Records*)

Andy Williams (left) and arranger Bob Mersey listen to a playback of their last take in the control booth. (*Columbia Records*)

Dick Jacobs conducts while Jackie Wilson sings. Jacobs, now an executive producer for Decca Records, was an early champion of rock-and-roll. (*Decca Records*)

5 COUNTRY AND WESTERN

They were called Scotch-Irish and they came at the end of the eighteenth century, after most of the good land along the Atlantic tidal plains had been divided up among the aristocratic families that comprised a New World landed gentry. So they pushed west and settled in the mountains that stretch from Pennsylvania south into Georgia. They carved small farms out of the forested valleys and the sides of rocky hills. They farmed, hunted, cut timber, mined coal, and distilled a potent whisky.

Then, history passed them by. A growing nation sprawled over their mountains and spread westward to the plains beyond and even to the shores of the Pacific. Cut off by inaccessible hills and valleys, proud and aloof, the mountain people who stayed behind developed a society in isolation. This society evolved around family clans and small mountain farms. It drew upon a fundamentalist, fire-and-brimstone religion and retained the manners and speech of eighteenth-century Scotland and Ireland. It also retained an Old World musical tradition.

Theirs was a music of ballads that told stories of ill-fated lovers, tragic heroes, of everyday work and problems, in simple, lilting melody. It was a music of wild reels and foot-thumping jigs. Its instruments were the dulcimer, the guitar, the fiddle, and, later, the banjo. But most of all it was a music of song, of tales told in melody.

When this music went west and north along with the mountain folk who followed the course of history, it changed. In the north it became the song of the lumberjacks, or shanty boys, as they were also called. The very word came from the French *chanter*—to sing—and song was the indispensable accompaniment to the ax.

The songs of the shanty boy were about the experiences of his everyday life. "A Shantyman's Life" celebrated the rigors of his daily routine; "The Little Brown Bulls" told of his work on the river; "The Logger's Boast" reflected his pride in his work; "The Jam on Gerry's Rock" described a log jam, the dread of all lumberjacks. These songs were filled with loneliness, bleakness, and nostalgia for home.

The opening of the West brought still another change to the mountain ballad. These were created by the cowboy in response to the conditions of his life. A simple person, close to the fundamentals of living and working, the cowboy sang songs that were simple in design and structure with little variety in rhythm, meter, and harmonic structure. He was a lonely man and his songs overflowed with yearning for home, a girl, peace. His best friend was his horse, and his greatest dread was a lonely grave. He sang about both. He also sang about breaking loose in Abilene or Dodge City. When he was sad, he lamented dying alone and being buried in a solitary grave on the endless prairie.

Some of the Scotch-Irish went to sea and here the ballad became the *chantey*—the sailor's song. Here, again, music played an indispensable role. The sailor needed song as much as he needed fresh water to see him through the long days at sea.

Chanteys fall into four rough categories, each derived from the type of work they were designed to accompany. Songs for jobs calling for short, heavy pulls were called "short drags." They had abrupt rhythms and crisp accents —as in "Haul Away, Joe" or "Haul in the Bowline." Songs for more sustained or heavier tasks such as hoisting sail or weighing anchor were called "halliards." For still more monotonous jobs there were "capstans," with long sustained melodies and slow, march-like rhythms. Finally, there were "foc'sle songs." These were not work songs, but songs designed for entertainment when the crew was off duty; songs about ladies of easy virtue, epics of whaling and fishing, ballads about sea heroes.

In the Appalachian highlands, however, the Scotch-Irish ballad was preserved in a pure form. The mountain communities remained isolated from the rest of the country. Then, the twentieth century reached into the mountain retreats. Roads were built through the valleys. Railroads carried the produce of farm and mine, along with the people, into the rest of the country. World War II called the men down from the hills to fight in Europe and the South Pacific. Finally, radio came and sets appeared in the small wooden farmhouses, and the mountain people were no longer isolated. The world had reached into their remote fastness and they reached out to the world.

The world also began to notice their music. In 1904, Emma Bell Miles described this music in an article titled "Some Real American Music" that appeared in *Harper's Magazine*. She called it a peculiarly American expression, a music that would repay serious study.

But outside of a few scholars and musicologists who studied this subculture, little was heard of this music by the nation at large for the next twenty years. Then, in the mid 1920's, a number of developments occurred that were to completely alter the status of mountain music. First, a radio station was constructed in Nashville, Tennessee, in 1925. Then, commercial recording companies discovered the substantial public response to mountain ballads and reels. Finally, Hollywood Westerns—with their inevitable guitar strumming and singing heroes—became a mainstay of the movie industry. All of these factors were to exert a powerful influence on the subsequent development of country and western music.

The Nashville radio station has probably provided the single strongest impetus for the development of this music. Radio station WSM—the call letters stand for "We Shield Millions," the slogan of the National Life and Accident Insurance Company, which built and owns the station— spawned a radio program that is, in the words of an official booklet, "the only radio program in the world that has never had a summer replacement, never had an intermission, never missed a performance since it started in 1925." The name of this program: *Grand Ole Opry.*

It all began in a small Nashville radio studio late in November 1925, when a bearded old fiddler named "Uncle" Jimmy Thompson sat down in front of a circular carbon microphone and proceeded to play. Station WSM was presenting its first *Barn Dance* show, the brain child of its musical director, ex-newsman George D. Hay.

That night, "Uncle Jimmy," eighty-one years old at the time, scraped out an hour's worth of reels, jigs, breakdowns, and sentimental ballads. After a few minutes, requests for specific songs began to come in to the studio by wire and telephone. The public which had tuned in to the program responded enthusiastically. About the only one who was not completely satisfied with the results was old Uncle Jimmy, who complained that "a man can't hardly get warmed up in an hour."

The show, which was to be renamed *Grand Ole Opry* two years later, was an immediate hit. It was to become the grand old man of American broadcasting, the longest continuous program in entertainment history that still reaches some ten million listeners every week. It provided an important showcase for country talent on a national scale.

George D. Hay, originator of the program, had been a reporter for *The Commercial Appeal* of Memphis, Tennessee, when he took the job as musical director of the new radio station in 1925. According to Hay, the original idea for *Grand Ole Opry* derived from an assignment given him by his newspaper a few years earlier to cover the funeral of an Ozark Mountain World War I hero.

After covering the funeral, Hay was invited to attend

a hoedown organized by the hero's neighbors to celebrate the funeral. "In an old barn, lighted by a coal-oil lamp in one corner," Hay later described the event, "they carried on till the crack of dawn. No one ever had more fun than those Ozark mountaineers had that night. It stuck with me until the idea became the *Grand Ole Opry* some seven years later."

On the program Hay himself took the part of the "solemn old judge," though he was only thirty years old at the time. He introduced the performers and provided a running commentary on the proceedings. This formula of country music together with homespun commentary proved to be a potent combination as far as the public was concerned.

The response was immediate. Before the first program signed off, its sponsors knew that they had a hit. The station was bombarded with phone calls and telegrams from listeners who requested favorite tunes or just wanted the people in charge to know how much they enjoyed the music. More amazing than this public response was the attraction the program had for country musicians and singers of all kinds. Fiddlers, banjo players, guitarists, drummers, singers, swarmed to station WSM wanting no more than an opportunity to perform on the air.

In the beginning the show was primarily instrumental, relying on such musicians as Uncle Jimmy Thompson on the fiddle accompanied by guitar, banjo, bass, and washboard. Then, in 1926, a singer who became famous as the "Dixie Dewdrop" joined the program as a regular member of the staff. His name was "Uncle" Dave Macon and he proved to be a star attraction as well as a colorful figure in his own right.

Both summer and winter Uncle Dave wore the same clothes—a double-breasted black jacket, striped pants, a wide-brimmed black felt hat and "gates ajar" collar. Indeed, Uncle Dave's sartorial elegance set a standard that is still emulated by country and western singers. For fifteen years the "Dixie Dewdrop" was one of the show's biggest attractions.

Today, *Grand Ole Opry* is held in a former tabernacle in Nashville and has grown into a four-and-a-half-hour marathon. More than five thousand people jam the hall when the program is presented on Saturday night to watch the seemingly chaotic production. Because of this overflow interest, there is now a Friday night Opry as well. As a tourist attraction, the program ranks with some of our national monuments and parks, drawing literally millions of visitors to Nashville each year. Among its many stars have been such popular country and western entertainers as Hank Snow, Ernest Tubbs, Cousin Minnie Pearl, Roy Acuff, Webb Pierce, Eddy Arnold, Tex Ritter, the Carter family, Bill Monroe, Flatt and Scruggs, Jimmie Rodgers, Pete Drake, and Johnny Cash—just to name a few.

The Opry is significant in the history of country and western music primarily because it brought to Nashville the leading talents in the complex and surprisingly varied field of country music. As performed on the program, this genre embraces such different musical forms as ballads, heart songs, honky-tonk, blue grass and western, train songs, breakdowns, fiddle and guitar tunes, hoedowns and novelty songs, topical satire, and plain country "corn."

Nashville's radio station WSM, however, cannot take all the credit for the renaissance of country music. Starting in the late 1920's, disk jockeys on stations throughout the South and the Midwest began to air this type of music. Then, from the 1930's on, hundreds of radio stations from Kentucky to the West Coast and south to Texas were broadcasting a steady diet of country and western music.

At the same time, record companies were discovering an important market for this music and proceeded to satisfy this substantial demand. When the depression of the 1930's brought the record industry practically to a halt, country and western records maintained a fairly steady sales figure. The country market proved to be more durable than some of the more fashionable types of popular music. At this time, however, record sales—even country and western sales —were by no means spectacular. A record that sold 10,000 copies during this period was considered a smash hit, and there were more hits among country and western records than in any other kind of music.

This steady market encouraged record makers. During the late 1920's and early 1930's, commercial producers scoured the countryside in order to put country music on wax. They traveled to hamlets, farms, mountain cabins, rural churches—anywhere that there was a fiddler or singer of note. They carried their rough recording equipment on horse, "Tin Lizzie," on foot, and even on mule. The result was what one commentator described as "the finest body of ethnic musical material ever collected."

One of the outstanding pioneers in the field was the late Ralph Peer, who worked both in country and Negro music. He originated the term "race" records and is credited with the discovery of Jimmie Rodgers, one of the all-time favorite country and western singers.

During this period record companies began building their country catalogues—a process that continues to this day. The sale of these records, however, was aimed primarily at the country market, which was ignored by the industry— and the nation—as a whole. It was not until the late 1930's, when country and western music had proved to be one of the mainstays of the popular-music industry, that the field began to command notice.

At first, this notice was hardly flattering. Country and western music was treated as an object for jokes and ridicule. Its leading practitioners were pictured as freakish, suspendered gawks with guitars singing odd songs with a nasal diction. It is an attitude that still persists in some urban circles.

The third great influence on the development of country and western music came with the Hollywood Western. By the early 1930's, the "horse opera" had become a staple of the industry and the studios turned out a steady stream of western epics. No less important to the genre than the horse was the singing, guitar-strumming hero. These films gave birth to such popular singing stars as Gene Autry, Tex Ritter, and Roy Rogers. Almost all of these "cowpunching" heroes began as singers rather than horsemen.

Gene Autry, for example, began his career with a fifteen-minute radio show on KVOO in Tulsa, Oklahoma, in 1928. He also began recording for Velvet Tone, a subsidiary of Columbia Records, that same year. His popularity as a singer in no way detracted from his popularity as a Western star, and his popularity crossed all regional and sectional lines.

"Even in the early days," Autry was recently quoted in *Billboard*, "there were just as many so-called 'pop' fans who thoroughly enjoyed country and western music as there are now. I do not agree with the idea that there is a wider interest in country and western music today than there was in the earlier years. I feel that there always was a strong following for this music from all walks of life."

Recording in Nashville began in the spring of 1945, when Decca Records ran a session with Red Foley. Before this time, most country and western recordings were made in the "field." Rural musicians and singers were recorded in impromptu studios set up in hotel rooms and country schoolhouses. Occasionally, performers were brought to studios in New York and Chicago to make records.

Following the lead of Decca in the late 1940's, every major label set up facilities in Nashville. The popularity of country music could no longer be ignored and since Nashville with its *Grand Ole Opry* was already a center, it became a logical site for country and western recording facilities.

The Nashville recording center has been growing steadily ever since that auspicious beginning. Today, Record Row, or Music City Boulevard, as it is alternately called, is a gleaming thoroughfare lined with new studios and publishing offices. The music industry has become the city's leading employer with upward of five thousand people—musicians, singers, composers, managers, technicians, and so on—supported directly and thousands more indirectly by the spinning disk. Nashville itself has become the third largest recording center in the country, ranking just below New York City and Los Angeles.

Nothing so clearly demonstrates the fact that the Nashville music boom is no temporary phenomenon as the fact that within the past few years Columbia, Capitol, and R.C.A. have invested over two million dollars in studio facilities in this hub of country sound. All three companies have bright new facilities on Nashville's Record Row.

Today, country and western music provides a major part of popular musical consumption in the United States, Canada, and abroad, especially in Germany, Japan, and South Africa. In a recent survey, *Cash Box*, a record industry journal, estimated that "Nashville based publishers, artists and record companies are directly involved with at least 20 per cent of the nation's top fifty best-selling singles."

This $100,000,000-a-year enterprise is based almost solely on a type of music and song whose derivation can be traced to Elizabethan England. The tradition has, of course, changed and evolved over the years until today country and western encompasses a surprising variety of musical forms and styles. It consists of old English ballads, cowboy songs, rural humor, religious songs, country blues, topical songs, work songs, bluegrass, honky-tonk. It passes into folk music and out of it.

Country music is actually a distinctive sound, a way of singing, and a special feeling for instrumentation. The subject matter of a song may vary, but you will rarely hear sophisticated lyrics or a sophisticated style of singing. At its best, we find in this music a closeness to reality, a willingness to face real problems head on, less fantasy and more honesty in dealing with such real life problems as poverty, death, love, and rejection.

Rural isolation has, of course, been all but ended. With modern mass-communication media the most isolated hamlet is just a switch away from the world at large. It is not surprising that country music has been affected by urban sophistication. This influence is reflected in the slick sounds of contemporary country music: violins, vocal groups, even brass and reeds are now used in country and western arrangements. But despite this influence, mainstream country music remains a musical language apart, a language that appears to speak with particular force to people overseas. Many a western European will know more about the songs of Buck Owens than he will of Frank Sinatra.

Despite its commercial success both nationally and internationally, country music is still somewhat of an underdog art form battling for acceptance. This battle is played out against the old stereotypes about hillbillies, rubes, corny humor, and sentimental lyrics. In the hubbub, musical values are ignored. Bluegrass has developed into an exciting jazzlike expression of distinctive charm and drive. The ballads and "heart songs" of such honky-tonk singers as Buck Owens and George Jones have a modern troubadour quality.

Country and western songwriters such as Harland Howard, John Loudermilk, and Merle Travis are keeping alive the ballad tradition of social commentary. At their best, these songs retain the tradition of honesty and meaningful treatment of real contemporary problems. Harlan Howard's poignant "Busted," for example, has been successfully recorded by both Burl Ives and Ray Charles, while Merle Travis's "Sixteen Tons" has achieved the status of a standard in the folk-music repertoire.

The work songs performed by such singers as Dave Dudley and Dick Curless provide a modern version of the lone man pitted against the occupational dangers of a hostile world. Roger Miller, whose whimsical humor and infectious tunes have brought him to national popularity, is assuming the stature of a Will Rogers with the added attraction of music.

Undoubtedly, Nashville and the music that stems from that center warrant serious attention. It provides voices and sounds that can be listened to with satisfaction by those for whom Andy Williams and Tony Bennett hold no interest.

More important, possibly, is the influence that country and western music has exerted in the great musical shout of the 1960's. Rock-and-roll—the dominant pop idiom of our time—is largely the result of a merger of white country singing with Negro rhythm and blues. All the leading figures in the early stages of rock-and-roll started as country singers, among them such outstanding influences as Chuck Berry, Elvis Presley, Carl Perkins, the Everly Brothers, Bill Haley, and Buddy Holly.

6 ROCK-AND-ROLL

Every generation discovers and nurtures a musical style that becomes identified as being peculiarly its own—a music that breaks sharply with the traditions of the past. This music generally takes on a form that is connected with what "respectable" elements of society describe as "wild, abandoned" dancing. If we look back at the history of popular music since the turn of the century, this pattern becomes obvious.

In the beginning, there was ragtime and its dance equivalents, the cakewalk and the foxtrot, which assumed the proportions of a national mania. In the 1920's, an earthy, vigorous jazz beguiled a generation and "flaming youth" were doing the charleston and the black bottom. In the latter half of the 1930's, swing came in the wake of the driving rhythm of the big band. Flaming youth became "jitterbugs" and the strenuous and athletic lindy hop and big apple dominated the dance floors. During the 1940's and 1950's, Latin American rhythms invaded the country, creating a vogue for the samba, the cha-cha, and the pachanga.

In each case, both music and dance began in the underground. They evolved in dance halls, honky-tonks, and cabarets, where the patrons were ready and willing to accept something a little more earthy and vital than what was available in the prevailing mode of the moment. In each case the music and dance exploded beyond its original confines to sweep across barriers of class and custom. In each case, this development was looked down on by conventional people as "amoral, degenerate frenzy."

It is hard to believe that the waltz was considered scandalous when it was first introduced at the end of the eighteenth century. At the time, polite society refused to condone such a barbaric dance and social arbiters were adamant in the opinion that the waltz would never replace the courtly minuet. The minuet was replaced, and the scandalous waltz became respectable.

A similar situation occurred in the late 1950's. A new kind of music erupted onto the scene, together with a new kind of dance. Within a relatively short time this new sound spread, took fire, until today it has become the dominant sound in popular music. Its dance equivalent has also swept up all the styles of the past, making even the lindy hop appear quaint and archaic.

The factors that determined the creation of the great

shout of the 1960's are many and complex. It would be all
but impossible to define them with any degree of completion. We can, however, trace the broad outlines of this development and get some idea of its history. We can begin
with the change that occurred in jazz during the latter part
of the 1930's. Jazz was absorbed into the big-band sound and
lost its spontaneous spirit. Huge bands, as we have seen,
took the jazz of improvisation and forced it into the rolling
beat of swing.

Spontaneity and individual invention were subordinated
to the sonorous richness of the heavy orchestration. The
music of the big bands progressed steadily along tracks
that were as carefully planned and arranged as those of
any railroad. Their sound was lush and polished, leaning
heavily on brass and massed saxophones. Constant Lambert,
the English conductor-composer and musicologist, suggests
in his book *Music Ho!* that this development was a popular
response to the highbrow richness of the Ravel-Delius period
in classical music.

Another factor was the improvement in recording techniques which permitted the accurate reproduction of the
rich sonorities of the big-band orchestration. For whatever
reason, the big band and swing represented the only nationally popular music of the late 1930's, 1940's, and, before
the rock-and-roll revolution, 1950's.

But brilliant, slick, and beautiful as the big band undoubtedly was, its music began to become arid once it lost
the creative heart that was rooted in jazz. Swing, as generated by the big bands, was completely opposed to the
spontaneous, improvisational spirit of jazz. There was no
place for free individual expression in its complex and
musically sophisticated arrangements.

Real jazz, meanwhile, had taken a different turn in the road. The post-war period saw a return to the small, intimate ensemble and the old New Orleans tradition of improvisation. Here, however, all resemblance ended. Originally, jazz had been the music for a vigorous and earthy dance style and was performed by musicians of genius who, nevertheless, were musically illiterate.

The new jazz was taking this classic improvisational style down unexpected bypaths. Jazz became a sophisticated lady. Ignoring the traditional association with dance, these new performers burst into abstract patterns of sound. In a way, they cut down to the heart of jazz, but at the same time they were doing something strange. What they performed was for listening only. Their music became "cool" and revealed a kind of Bauhaus purity of expression.

Then, as the progressive jazzmen went further in their exploration of the improvisational art, their music became even more abstract. Finally it resembled nothing so much as a sound version of what the abstract expressionists were doing in painting. The dance was completely forsaken in the interest of sound.

The big band found itself in creative crisis. Cut off from its heart in a more earthy form of jazz, its sound was degenerating into a vapid, Muzak-like ooze of notes. The major sources of hits during this period were coming from three areas: Broadway shows, Hollywood musicals, and the novelty factories of Tin Pan Alley. It was a bleak period for popular music.

At the same time, however, another kind of music was bubbling in the hinterlands. In fact, there were a number of musical styles, and, occasionally, examples would sneak onto the record charts. There was rhythm and blues—a type of music that was for the most part limited to the Negro community; there was country and western, a style sneered at as "hillbilly" by knowing city folk; and there was gospel —Negro church music sung with powerful rhythm and equally powerful emotional drive. All of these were to play significant roles in the development of rock-and-roll.

During this period a folk-music trend was also beginning to show signs of growth. At first, it was ethnically oriented and leaned heavily on such esoterica as the harvest songs of Moldavia and romantic ballads from the Dutch moors. It was very much a specialty, confined mainly to college campuses and a few far-out coffee houses in Greenwich Village and San Francisco.

For a time, leftist-oriented folk music enjoyed a vogue. The hootenanny comes from this period, along with preference for guitarist-singers clad in work shirts and a repertoire that included songs from the Spanish civil war and ballads celebrating the struggles of the C.I.O. during the union's formative years. This phase was almost squashed with the repression that came with the McCarthy era, a period whose influence was felt in all forms of creative endeavor.

It was out of a synthesis of these different kinds of music that the earthy, vital sound of our time was to evolve. The process was slow and gradual. Jazz, as we have seen, became big-band on the one hand, and esoteric on the other. In both cases it lost its root appeal. Then, rhythm and blues burst on the scene, and when it absorbed gospel, country and western, and folk, it became rock-and-roll and outranked everything else.

First, it was Deep South, or country, blues with a heady

admixture of the massive rhythms of gospel. Then came the electric guitars, the high, amplified sound with a generous dose of country and western. In the late 1940's and early 1950's, Chuck Berry, Bo Diddley, Muddy Waters and John Lee Hooker were making records that were gaining vociferous admirers.

In the industry, most of these disks were referred to as "race" records. That is, they were made primarily by and for Negroes. They were, however, played over the air—featured by Negro disk jockeys on Negro programs—and anyone could tune in to a radio station. It soon became evident that droves of teen-agers—Negro and white—were turning to the "race" stations. Here they discovered a sound that communicated.

In Cleveland, an enterprising young disk jockey named Alan Freed was also listening. Tentatively, he began to play some of these recordings on his own programs. He called this music "rock-and-roll." The response was quick and dramatic and Freed's audience grew in direct proportion to the number of rock-and-roll selections he featured on his programs.

That was the beginning. The new sound, originating in the "race" stations, caught on and spread. The first important breakthrough came in 1954, when a number of songs performed by a group called the Crows rocketed to the top of the charts. The Crows sang a modified version of rhythm and blues in the three records that figured in this early breakthrough: "Hucklebuck," "Long Gone," and "Pink Champagne."

The reaction of the musical establishment was typical. All the powers that be in the pop-music world—radio stations, big record companies, Hollywood, television, song publishers—were unanimous in their condemnation. "Junk," they called this new sound and attributed its popularity to a freak craze. Many radio stations refused to play the new music, and the big record companies and song publishers simply ignored it.

Despite this opposition, the popularity of rock-and-roll kept right on growing. Here was a music that had captured the fancy of the public with only limited exposure through the mass media. Despite its success, the musical establishment chose to ignore rock-and-roll. Its popularity, however, kept right on growing.

One of the more persistent myths of our time describes rock-and-roll as a synthetic product foisted on a gullible public through shrewd and cynical manipulation of public taste. The truth of the matter, as can be verified by a brief review of the facts, is that exactly the opposite happened. The taste makers and manipulators missed this boat. They fought rock-and-roll all along the line of its development, finally capitulating only when they realized that their old stock in trade no longer had a market.

The veracity of this view is demonstrated by the fact that the big record companies—Columbia, R.C.A. Victor, Capitol, and Decca—sat on the sidelines as passive spectators. Small companies took the chances with unknown performers and a new kind of music. Small companies made the records and promoted the vocal groups that were to give shape to the music of the 1960's. It is only during the past few years that the big companies have begun to jump on the bandwagon.

An additional impetus to the growing popularity of rock-

and-roll came, indirectly, from television. After World War II, the television industry mushroomed, achieving a dominant position in home entertainment by the late 1940's and early 1950's. The big programs switched from radio to the home screen, leaving behind a vacuum in both programs and profits.

This situation created a crisis in radio. The vacuum had to be filled. Radio stations tried desperately to hold on to a diminishing audience. Talk programs, interviews, news broadcasts, contests, personalities, topical discussions, and musical programs were tried in an attempt to lure the public away from the Cyclop's eye of the television screen. None of them worked very well, and it appeared that radio was all but doomed.

Then, however, came the transistorized portable radio that could be carried anywhere and everywhere—to beaches, to picnics, on the street, all places where television could not follow. Along with the portable radio came rock-and-roll. Radio stations all over the country programmed diskjockey shows that featured the new sounds. This exposure created new fans and the process repeated itself, resulting in the resurgence of radio and a huge jump in record sales.

Another, equally important factor in this development was the technical ease with which a recording could be made. With the magnetic tape recorder, it became a comparatively easy and inexpensive process. Practically anyone with an idea or a new song concept could have his brain child translated into a tangible recorded product. Hundreds of small record companies came into being and a mad scramble for playing time on radio began.

This situation was described in *Cash Box*:

Formerly, to get a good sounding record, a producer had to gather a group of skilled musicians, a top arranger, and an experienced singer. Today, that is no longer necessary. A producer can go into a tiny studio with the author usually singing his own songs accompanied by himself or a small group and come out with a "side" which, while it might not measure up to mature musical standards, nevertheless has the appeal to sell—and sell in quantity to the teen age market. . . .

But the emergence of rock-and-roll into a dominant position in popular music was not an overnight occurrence. The musical establishment resisted the change. The surging market was brushed off as a temporary phenomenon, something that would pass in the night. Even when Bill Haley's "Rock Around the Clock" started its climb onto the record charts in 1954 and went on to become the best-selling non-seasonal record of all time with a total sale to date of more than fifteen million, rock-and-roll was still looked on as a passing fad. Critics dismissed the genre as musical dross, convinced that its primitive rhythms, wailing singing styles, and melodic simplicity could never sustain prolonged interest—even among teen-agers.

Then, in 1956, a new singer erupted onto the scene. He came out of country and western, with a liberal admixture of rhythm and blues and something of the gospel spirit mingled in a wild, emotion-charged singing style that communicated to teen-agers all over the world. His name was Elvis Presley.

What Presley did was produce a new synthesis that was so potent that millions of teen-agers all over the world hailed it as the voice of their generation. His "Heartbreak Hotel" was number one on all three lists—country and western, rhythm and blues, and pop. This was the first time anything like this had happened. Presley's popularity cut across racial, regional, and ethnic boundaries, and his recordings obliterated the lines that separated the different categories of pop music. The wall that the musical establishment had erected began to crumble.

The breach was widened further by the efforts of an enterprising, young producer from Philadelphia named Phil Spector. Uncannily sensitive to the mood of his generation, Spector produced a string of hit records that dominated the charts during the late 1950's and early 1960's. Taking full advantage of electronic recording techniques, Spector's records were assaults on the ear. He perfected the techniques of over-dubbing and electronically manipulated sound, producing a new kind of recording style that brought the inherent vigor and vitality of rock-and-roll into sharp focus.

Despite the success of Presley, Spector, and other rock-and-roll performers, the genre was still considered nothing more than a teen-age craze. An additional element was needed to make the conquest of the musical establishment complete. A dance form that corresponded to the music had not, as yet, evolved. Teen-agers danced to the songs of Elvis Presley and other early rock-and-roll records, but their dance was nothing more than a modified version of the lindy.

The lindy hop, however, was expressive of swing. It grew out of the big band sound of the late 1930's and 1940's. It reflected the powerful, ordered rhythms of its musical counterpart. In the lindy, movements and steps are circumscribed within a recognizable and ordered routine. Rock-and-roll was something else and demanded a new dance concept before it could really take the world by storm.

This concept came in the late 1950's, developing in many

places throughout the country where teen-agers abandoned themselves to the driving rhythms of rock-and-roll. It came to a head with the famed twist, as popularized by Chubby Checker, Joey Dee, and other rock-and-roll performers at that time. The new dance was, actually, no dance at all in the sense of an orderly progression of movements—a characteristic of all past popular dance styles.

Instead, the twist was anarchy. Its execution demanded nothing more than an uninhibited abandon to the rhythm of the music. There was nothing to learn, nothing to do. There were no partners and no recognizable steps. All the dancer need do was twist in time to the music.

With the twist, the adult world discovered the new sound. Overnight, discotheques appeared all over the world where everyone—from high society to suburban matrons—came for an evening of sensual abandonment. The twist spread like a wave, engulfing all segments of the population. So warmly have adults embraced the teen beat, that an estimated 40 per cent of the top rock-and-roll hits are bought by people over twenty years old. A New York rock-and-roll station estimates its adult audience at substantially more than 50 per cent.

With the twist, all the walls came tumbling down. The big record companies, no longer able to ignore the writing on the wall, began to compete for big-name rock-and-roll performers. The big beat was big business. As a result, performances became more professional and polished. The rock-and-roll idiom was refined and perfected when such talented arrangers as Burt Bacharach, Bob Mersey, Don Costa, Marty Manning, Bert Keyes, and others applied their talents and skills to its creation.

Following in the wake of the twist, as though confirming the status of the new sounds, came the unprecedented invasion from England. First, there were the Beatles—a foursome of long-haired, outspoken, joyous young musicians with electronic instruments that made echo chambers seem old hat and songs that struck joy into the heart of the world.

The Beatles were followed by shock troops from Manchester, London, the Midlands that called themselves the Rolling Stones, the Animals, the Dave Clark Five, Herman's Hermits, and Gerry and the Pacemakers among others. Until only a little while ago, it was this British sound that dominated American radio and popularity charts.

Dick Jacobs, of Decca Records, traces this outpouring of British music to the phenomenal success of two American groups that toured England in 1958. "That year," Jacobs said, "Buddy Holly and the Everly Brothers toured England. Their reception was phenomenal. Everywhere they appeared, crowds of young English boys and girls packed the halls. They listened and imitated. In teen-age cellar clubs in London, Liverpool, Manchester, all over England, performers reacted to this influence. There were, of course, other influences, but I cannot help but feel that Buddy Holly and the Everly Brothers were decisive. You can still hear traces of their styles in the performances of practically every important rock-and-roll group from England."

This English dominance was finally challenged by two new American developments. The first was the emergence of folk-rock, a synthesis of folk music and rock-and-roll. This style combines the ballad-like quality of folk song with the rhythmic, instrumental, and vocal inventions of rock-and-roll. The most important contribution of folk-rock, however, lies in its lyric content and treatment. Eschewing the "June-Moon" clichés of the traditional Tin Pan Alley song, folk-rock brings lyrics of remarkable sensitivity and perception to contemporary popular music.

Spearheaded by the creative outpouring and commercial success of Bob Dylan—who began his career as an ethnically oriented folk singer—folk-rock confronts the most important issues of our time. Dylan's songs, whose poetry reveals near genius, have raised rock-and-roll to the level of significant commentary. His songs range from a gentle, somewhat sardonic satire of the old love-ballad clichés, as in "It Ain't Me Babe," to an eloquent plea for social justice in "Blowin' in the Wind"; from a condemnation of that blind, super-patriotism which finds expression in war—"With God on Our Side" and "Masters of War"—to an examination of the relationship between the generations in "The Times They Are A-Changin'."

When we sought to reprint some of Dylan's lyrics, we were confronted by the specter of business—whose relationship to popular music was discussed in Chapter 1. The publisher refused to grant permission. We had naïvely considered Dylan's poetry a national treasure—something on the order of the Grand Canyon or the Statue of Liberty. But the publisher regards them as a valuable property.

A number of talented performers and composers have broadened the expressive potential of folk-rock. Among them have been Barry McGuire, whose emotion-charged performance of "Eve of Destruction" climbed to the top of the lists; the Lovin' Spoonful; the Byrds; Sonny and Cher; Simon and Garfunkel, whose songs—written by Paul Simon—evoke the haunting melancholy and alienation of the contemporary world; and the precocious—"out of the mouths of babes"—Janis Ian.

There have, of course, always been songs of social protest and serious commentary on the problems that plague the world. These, however, have rarely entered the mainstream of the commercial currents of popular music, and have generally been relegated to the fringe areas of hootenanny sing-outs, college campuses, and coffeehouses. Folk-rock, on the other hand, has won a niche among the most popular elements of contemporary music. Songs from the style consistently appear at the top of the charts. They are played on the radio and folk-rock records are bought by the millions. One wonders what effect these songs, most of which are inspired by and express the highest ideals, will have on the millions of teenagers who listen to them so avidly.

The second challenge to the British dominance came from a record company in Detroit, Michigan, called appropriately, Mo-Town. Mo-Town records specialize in "soul" music as performed by such outstanding groups as the Supremes and the Four Tops. Their records have introduced or rather reintroduced, a pure rhythm and blues style— the kind of thing that was once called "race" or "brown sound" and the kind of thing that started it all to begin with.

Rock-and-roll has demonstrated America's continuing ability to create a music to which the people of the world can respond. Today, it provides the distinctive sound of our time and generation and its popularity has swept the world. In one respect, this popularity represents a musical regression in taste. Rock-and-roll takes its drive and impetus from the earliest, most primitive forms of country and western, rhythm and blues, and gospel singing. In a more important respect, rock-and-roll has been a potent liberating force in popular music.

In its wake, all the clichés of the older ballad, jazz, and swing styles, both instrumental and vocal, have been swept away. Because it breaks so radically with tradition, rock-and-roll has evolved a whole new vocabulary of performance techniques. It exploits the voice, for example, in totally novel and unexpected ways, raising the glissando, speech, and falsetto to new levels of expressiveness.

Instrumental innovations in rock-and-roll have generated novel, unorthodox patterns while the unabashed utilization of electronic instruments and techniques has irrevocably upset the old instrumental band and orchestra balances. In rock-and-roll the harmonic progression of the song becomes allied directly with the straightforward, driving rhythms and exploits harmonic combinations that were studiously avoided in the past.

The result is a musical form that combines the earthiness and vigor of the earliest jazz styles with the advanced techniques of modern electronics. Out of these combinations has come a driving, pulsating musical style that has captured the imagination of the world. The extent of this dominance is revealed in the casual street-corner singing of today's teenagers. Only ten years ago, this kind of singing was characterized by harmonization based upon the common triad. Today anything goes, and one hears the most outlandish combination of tones that range from parallel fifths to the most complex diminished seventh progressions —sounds that would have been dismissed as the worst kinds of dissonance only yesterday.

The vitality of the form is also attested to by the creativity it has generated. A whole generation of songwriters whose output rivals that of any other era, has come out of rock-and-roll. Certainly, the songs of John Lennon and Paul McCartney of Beatle fame compare favorably with those of any popular songwriting team in history.

Their compositions are characterized by a musical inventiveness that has extended the limits of popular music in every direction. In their songs odd rhythmic devices— abrupt, startling changes from 4/4 to 3/4 time, extended rubatos, alterations in meter—abound alongside daring harmonic progressions. Their instrumentation exploits musical resources never before utilized in popular music. In their search for a sound with which to beguile the ear of the listener, Lennon and McCartney have ranged over the complete spectrum of musical notation. The classic string quartet, baroque trumpets, the harpsichord, exotic instruments like the Indian sitar and tamboura, the electric organ, drums and percussive instruments of all kinds, and, of course, the amplified guitar, have all been utilized in Beatle songs in superbly integrated, spontaneous invention.

Rock-and-roll's vitality is also revealed in the new styles generated by the form. Probably the most important recent innovations are acid-rock and raga-rock. The principal development of acid-rock has been centered in the Haight-Ashbury area of San Francisco where the style grew out of the "hippie" community of non-conformist drop-outs from our aggressive, materialistic society. Here, such groups as the Grateful Dead, the Five Americans, and the Jefferson Airplane have exploited electronic sounds and instruments to produce an emotion-charged style that reflects the psychedelic experience. The Jefferson Airplane's hit single, "Somebody to Love," is typical of the style.

Acid-rock, however, has not been limited to the San Francisco groups. The influence of the style is widespread and is evident in the recordings made by such divergent groups as the Lovin' Spoonful, in their "Summer in the City" and "Darling Be Home Soon" and the Beatles with "Strawberry Fields Forever" and "Penny Lane."

Whereas acid-rock utilizes the most modern electronic innovations, raga-rock exploits the exotic sounds of such ancient instruments as the Indian sitar and tamboura, the Greek buzukie and santuri, the Arabic oud, and the Turkish cymbalom. In raga-rock melodies tend to fall into the pentatonic scale typical of Near Eastern folk music. Most notable of the recent examples of this style have been: "Paint It Black" and "Mother's Little Helper" sung by the Rolling Stones, "Tomorrow Never Knows" by the Beatles, and "Bang, Bang" by Sonny and Cher.

The new Bohemian underground has also found a voice in rock-and-roll in the guise of a nihilistic, irreverent, long-haired, electronic-instrumented group that calls themselves the Fugs. Outspoken and savagely satirical, the songs of the group, which are often on the pornographic side, have been banned from the mass entertainment media. Despite this ban, however, the Fugs have enjoyed considerable underground success. They have been performing for the past few years in a Greenwich Village theater, and their albums sell consistently in the 100,000 range.

Like so many earlier popular musical styles, rock-and-roll represents a synthesis of existing forms and modes. It is basically rhythm and blues with interpolations of country and western, gospel, and folk music. Rock-and-roll is as authentic a musical style as jazz or ragtime. Like its predecessors, it has emerged from obscure origins into international popularity.

For the past ten years this idiom has dominated popular music. During this period the style has been refined and perfected. Today its influence is felt in every aspect of the popular music field. This influence can be seen in the instrumental inventiveness of modern arrangements as well as in the increasing utilization of electronic sound manipulation. It is also evident in the singing styles of such non-rock-and-roll performers as Barbra Streisand, Lainie Kazan, and Andy Williams.

Like all popular musical styles, rock-and-roll is destined to pass from the scene. In time, it will be replaced by a new sound generated through the dynamics of a new generation. It will, however, never completely disappear. Just as rock-and-roll contains within itself traces of all the popular styles of the past, so will rock-and-roll's vigorous idiom have a place in the formulation of the next synthesis—the music of a new generation.

When it comes, let us approach it with something of the spirit of Bertrand Russell, who wrote almost fifty years ago: "In what is new and growing there is apt to be something crude, insolent, even a little vulgar, which is shocking to the man of sensitive taste; quivering from the rough contact, he retires to the trim gardens of the polished past, forgetting that they were reclaimed from the wilderness by men as rough and earth-soiled as those from whom he shrinks in his own day."

7 THE ARRANGER

He is the unsung hero of popular music. Outside of the industry hardly anyone knows his name, but within it everyone depends on him. Although anonymous, he provides the finished showcase that reaches the public ear. He is the arranger and his contribution is central to the creative drama that is popular music.

Creatively, he occupies a position somewhat below the original composer, but above the performer. For the most part he uses other people's material, yet he is an artist in his own right. Out of his imagination and skill he must fashion a musical environment in which artist and song may shine.

His raw material is a song, a thirty-two-bar construction of melody, lyrics, harmony, and rhythm. These must be molded into a vehicle that will highlight the approach, style, and voice quality of the individual singer or instrumentalist while remaining true to the "feel" of the original song. The arranger must be able to take an old war horse that has been performed endlessly and breathe new life and invention into its tired old bars.

It is estimated that a quarter of a million arrangements of popular songs and musical themes are prepared each year. These are utilized in every phase of popular music. They are used for recordings and night-club acts, for television spectaculars and theaters, for motion pictures and concert performances. Arranging has grown into an industry in itself and employs an army of musical journeymen who range from genuine creative talents to musical hacks. The directory of New York City's Local 802 (the musicians' union) lists some sixteen hundred arrangers.

Like so many other professionals in the world today, the arranger tends to specialize. As a result, there are all kinds practicing their craft. Some specialize in show music, providing a professional finish to the score of a musical comedy, others concentrate on jazz or folk music, while still others devote themselves to country and western, rock-and-roll, or romantic ballads. There are, however, a handful of all-purpose arrangers who will apply themselves to any and all popular genres.

Included in this latter category is Marty Manning, one of our more competent practitioners, who is at home in practically every phase of pop music. Tall, slim, with thinning red hair, angular features, and an affable manner, his credits run the gamut of popular musical expression. They range from rock-and-roll to romantic ballads, from big-band arrangements to commercial jingles, from background music for television shows to original songs.

"It's all music," Marty explains. "No matter how you slice it, the problem boils down to one thing—the creation of a sound that will communicate to the public."

This question of communication lies at the heart of the arranger's art. He must strike a balance between public preference and his own originality. The ability to do so is the measure of success and places heavy demands on the arranger's taste, judgment, and experience. Above all else, Manning's arrangements strike this balance. They are neither so far out as to alienate the listener, nor are they so far back as to bore him.

"Arranging," Manning says, "is always a compromise. You have to be original without being radical, daring but not foolhardy. The arranger writes for that nameless entity called the public, but can never make the mistake of writing down to them. When he does, the results are invariably disastrous."

Another characteristic of a Manning arrangement lies in his ability to tailor the musical material to the specific needs of the individual artist. His arrangements fit like a glove, highlighting a singer's strong points while obscuring his shortcomings.

In the course of a year, Manning will prepare charts (industry word for arrangements) for some two hundred songs, tailored to the needs of a dozen or more singers. Each artist presents a special problem. Before beginning a chart, Manning listens to the singer and carefully studies his style and voice quality. These factors will determine the "feel" of an arrangement. They will dictate the kind of harmonic and rhythmic treatment utilized as well as the instrumentation of the orchestral accompaniment.

"There is a lot an arrangement can do for a singer," Marty explains. "Let us say that a singer does not have a particularly accurate ear. The arranger can help by giving him orchestral harmonies that he can grab hold of and hang on to, that will bolster his ear. Another singer may be weak in the high register of his voice. Again, the arranger can help. He can, for example, beef up his high notes with a discreet doubling in the reeds or strings. Still another singer might have a powerful rhythmic sense. In such a case, the arrangement will be designed to focus upon and accent this ability."

At the same time, the arranger must consider the song he is working with. The melody, lyric treatment, and rhythm of the individual song must be balanced against the abilities and qualities of the singer. A further compromise is compelled by budgetary considerations, which will determine the size and instrumentation of the band that will be used. All these factors enter into the arrangement; each must be balanced against the others.

"An arrangement," Marty feels, "is nothing more than a showcase—an attractive frame for both singer and song. Ideally, it is a musical vehicle that enhances both. In preparing a chart, my own guiding principles are simplicity, technical perfection, and good taste."

To achieve these ends, Manning brings a lifetime of experience and a thorough musical training to the task. Born in Haverhill, Massachusetts, in 1916, to a family that was not particularly musical, Manning cannot remember a time when he was not fascinated by music. He began to study the violin when he was six years old and has been seriously involved with music ever since. In high school he taught a course in harmony to his fellow students, beginning in his sophomore year. After finishing high school, he won a scholarship to the New England Conservatory in Boston, where he continued his musical studies. From the beginning Manning's interest was focused on popular music.

"This was the music that was closest to me," he recalls. "This was the music I listened to and played and felt most comfortable with. This was the music that appealed to most people and this was the music I wanted to make."

After his graduation from the conservatory, Manning enrolled for additional courses at New York University, where he studied the Schillinger system of musical composition.

"I rarely use the system directly in arranging," Marty says, "but this knowledge provides an additional tool I can turn to when I feel the need for it. Harmony, counterpoint, even the twelve-tone system are all tools of the trade. These are the basic skills without which a composer or an arranger cannot function. Of course, a great deal of what you learn is simply ignored in your day-to-day work, but before you can break the rules, you have to know them."

All of Manning's schooling was directed toward mastery of the popular idiom. As a student, he had decided to make a career in popular music as an arranger and composer and prepared himself accordingly. He broke into professional arranging in New York City in 1939. "This was the era of the big band," Marty recalls, "and my first charts were prepared for the Bob Chester orchestra, which was featured in the *Band of the Week* program at the New Yorker Hotel."

Manning's abilities were soon recognized and for the next ten years he perfected his skills in a demanding professional world. He prepared charts for most of the "name" bands of the time and also did arrangements for singers, including a number for a young singer named Frank Sinatra, who was then appearing with the Tommy Dorsey orchestra. He was a staff arranger for the Mark Warnow *Hit Parade* orchestra and later for the Raymond Scott orchestra.

By the early 1950's, Manning had established what appeared to be a solid reputation in the industry. His abilities were widely appreciated and his arrangements were in demand. Then a series of mishaps brought his career to a temporary halt. They began with an accident in 1953. A pair of rimless glasses he had been wearing were broken and a sliver of glass cut his left eye. The cut drained all the fluid from his eye and doctors despaired of saving it. For eleven months, the eye failed to respond to treatment. Finally, vision returned and the eye began to mend, but then Manning suffered a detached retina.

"I was completely immobilized for four weeks," Marty recalls. "The doctors strapped me into a bed flat on my back. I had to lie absolutely still without moving a muscle. Both my eyes were covered with bandages."

When the retina had healed sufficiently for Manning to be able to move again, he had to relearn such simple functions as sitting and walking. For months after, he wore two cups over his eyes with only a pinhole in each one to admit light.

"I remember doing an awful lot of praying during this time," Marty said. "According to the doctors, it was touch and go all the way."

When his sight returned to normal and he was able to

get around once more, Marty faced a new problem. He confronted another very real aspect of the popular-music industry. He had been away from the scene for almost two years, and two years, he discovered, was a long time in the pop-music world.

"I was forgotten," Marty says ruefully. "It was a case of out of sight, out of mind. Things had changed. A new sound had developed and new people were making it. I was like a beginner again, starting at the bottom—except that I had a wife and three children to look after. Time and medical expenses had exhausted our savings. We were broke. So I did what every beginner has to do. I made the rounds looking for work and took anything that was offered."

Jackie Gleason gave him one of his first commissions. In 1955, Manning wrote the background music for *The Honey-mooners*. He also did some arrangements for the Percy Faith orchestra, but commissions were few and far between. Then, in 1957, Manning did the arrangements for a Vic Damone summer-replacement show on television. This was the beginning. The industry began to take notice and more commissions began to trickle in. When his arrangement of "I Left My Heart in San Francisco," which he prepared for Tony Bennett, climbed to the top of the charts early in 1962, all doors opened. Manning won the Grammy Award for that arrangement and his problems evaporated.

Today, Manning's arrangements are in demand and he is under constant pressure to complete charts for singers like Jerry Vale, Connie Francis, Robert Goulet, Tony Bennett, Phyllis Maguire, Vic Damone—to name just a few of the singers he has worked with.

"The pop-music field has changed considerably from the

time I began to write," Manning says. "It was much simpler then. You had the big band and this was the context in which you worked. You knew what each section of the band could do and wrote accordingly. Today, the arranger has almost complete freedom—a legacy of rock-and-roll. This freedom, however, is not an unmixed blessing. The arranger can, for example, use bass flutes, or an ocarina or an Indian sitar—instruments we would never dream of using in the old days. On the one hand, this freedom makes for a much more inventive and original sound. On the other, it makes heavy demands upon the originality and ingenuity of the arranger."

Marty works in a studio in his Huntington, Long Island, home that overlooks the Sound. He does most of his arranging at a four-octave harmonium.

"I like to be able to hear sustained chords," Marty explains. "This gives me a better idea of what the harmonies will sound like when they are performed."

A thorough professional with a solid musical background, Manning is dedicated to his craft. There is nothing he would rather do.

"When you can take an old war horse that has been performed sixteen zillion times," Marty says, "and manage to make it sound fresh and bright—that, my friend, is satisfaction."

An entirely different approach is taken by Bert Keyes, an arranger who is somewhat more of a specialist. We spoke to Bert in the offices of the Roosevelt Music Company, with which he is associated. Short, energetic, and intense, he described his attitudes toward his work and toward music in the pithy, slangy musical vernacular.

"Music," he says, "is my element, like water is to a fish. I've been involved with sound all my life. It's my thing. I think and feel in musical terms."

Rock-and-roll and jazz are Bert's preferred musical language. These are the forms he knows best and is most comfortable with. Unlike Manning, who prepared himself specifically for a career in arranging, Keyes came up through the ranks as a working musician. He began studying the piano when he was five years old and later learned the bass and vibraphone. He remembers entertaining at parties and informal gatherings before he was twelve, and by the time he was fifteen he was playing professionally in night clubs.

"I learned arranging through experience," Bert says. "When you perform in a club night after night, you have to be inventive. If you aren't, you're liable to bore yourself to death. Besides, there are people out there who came to hear you and you've got to give them something or else they're going to stop coming. In a way, the working musician, especially the jazz player, is always arranging. He is always looking for a new figuration or harmonic progression—a new sound—that will catch the ear of that public."

Bert's first arrangements were made for his own groups. He prepared material for night-club acts and for concert performances, for vocals and for straight instrumental numbers. Through this kind of practical experience Bert became familiar with all the instruments. He came to know the tonal potentiality of various instrumental combinations and learned how to use this potential to the full.

"An arrangement has got to be exciting," Bert says. "It makes no difference how this excitement is created. It can come from a single guitar chord or from sixteen trumpets blowing their brains out. If you can achieve it, you're *in.* If you can't, you're *out.*"

Bert is probably best known for his rock-and-roll arrangements with such vocal groups as the Marcels, the Shirelles, and the Crests. Among his credits is a record that this writer considers a masterpiece of the rock-and-roll genre. It is called "Mocking Bird" and is based on an old Kentucky mountain lullaby. As sung in a duet by Inez and Charlie Foxx, the lilting Elizabethan ballad is transfused with the rhythmic drive and the vitality of gospel and rhythm and blues.

Inez provides the lead voice, embroidering the melody with blue notes and supple rhythmic modifications. Charlie provides the "response" voice that answers the lead in a discreet duet that echoes and embroiders the lead voice. Both voices soar over and above a harmonic and rhythmic background provided by guitars, drums, and bass.

"This was actually a 'head' arrangement," Bert explains. "That is, there were no prepared charts for the session. We had lead sheets for the musicians and a pair of great singers. The arrangement was worked out right there in the studio. Inez has a powerful rhythmic feel and this provided the framework for the musical idea expressed in the record.

"In order to highlight this quality in Inez's singing, we developed a driving, steady rhythmic background. This provided the base from which Inez and Charlie could take off and return to in their performance. We fooled around with a number of different rhythmical figures before we hit on the right one. How did we know when we found it? That's hard to say. You feel it when it's right—in the pit of your stomach."

Most of Bert's arrangements, however, are more formal. That is, he prepares complete orchestrations beforehand. Although the bulk of his work has been involved with jazz and rock-and-roll, Keyes has also prepared arrangements for show tunes and standard ballads, including charts for such singers as Nat Cole, Dionne Warwick, and the Ames Brothers.

"In all cases," Bert says, "the problem is the same. What is music, after all? It's nothing more than a feeling expressed in sound. This idea or feel must be communicated to the listener, and in order to do so, it has got to be real. You can't fake it because the public just isn't about to buy a fake. The most important thing in arranging, in all music for that matter, is honesty. If you can put a real, honest feeling across, it has got to be good. If you can't, it has got to be bad, no matter how slick, professional, or technically perfect it may otherwise be."

This honesty is central to Bert's approach to music. It is reflected in his instrumental treatment, as it is in his acceptance of new musical ideas and styles.

"Music," Bert says, "is a living thing. It is always changing and developing. If you get hung up on yesterday's sound, your work has got to be fake. The arranger, ideally, is working on tomorrow's sound."

Whereas Bert Keyes and Marty Manning both decided on musical careers early in their lives, Peter Matz, another top-flight arranger, came to music through a more circuitous route. Peter is a chemical engineer with a degree from U.C.L.A. He became professionally involved with music, however, before he ever practiced engineering.

"Actually," Peter says, "I was always interested in music.

I studied the piano as a kid and later learned saxophone and clarinet. I worked my way through school as a musician— playing everything from club dates to Bar Mitzvahs."

Pursuing his interest in music, Matz played in the U.C.L.A. band, but did not decide to make music a profession until after he was graduated. After finishing school in 1950, Matz spent two years in Paris, where his instrumental abilities drew him into a musical circle. Most of his friends were musicians and composers and this association further influenced his decision.

"In Paris," Matz recalls, "I began studying music seriously for the first time. It was during this period that I finally decided on a career in music, though the idea had always been in the back of my mind. I felt that I was better suited temperamentally for a life in music than in engineering. I never regretted this decision."

After returning to New York in 1954, Matz continued his musical studies with Wallingford Riegger while supporting as a working musician and fledgling arranger. During this time he prepared arrangements for night club acts, individual singers, and for a Broadway musical. His most important break, however, came through the Perry Como television show for which he worked as rehearsal pianist. After preparing the arrangements for a number of production numbers, Matz was offered a position as staff arranger for the program.

"It was a question of being in the right place at the right time," Peter Matz maintains. "Fortunately, those first arrangements turned out well, and I was invited to prepare more."

From the beginning, Matz's arrangements were characterized by a sophisticated rhythmic and harmonic sensitivity that was timely and listenable—indispensable qualities for the pop arranger.

"It is difficult to explain what I do," Matz says. "Basically, my approach is instinctive. I find that the less I think about a chart, the better it turns out. It's a question of feeling, of how I hear a melody and how I react to the lyrics. Of course, you have to know what you are doing. You have to have some idea of harmonic structure and musical form. These factors, however, are secondary as far as my own work is concerned. The initial feeling, the instinctive impulse is the important thing. Everything else is nothing more than the means to an end."

Once the initial impulse has crystallized, Matz finds, the actual writing out of a chart proceeds easily. This approach is followed in all of his arrangements and his credits include examples from practically every aspect of pop music. He has, for example, prepared the arrangements for Barbra Streisand's very successful album, "People." He was musical director for the *Hullabaloo* television program and has written songs, commercial jingles, and the music for several television specials, including *Color Me Barbra,* an Edie Adams special, and *The Light Fantastic,* featuring Lauren Bacall.

"Each type of performance," Matz says, "presents its own problems. When you write for television, for example, the arrangements are different from those used for a record session. A record session offers the arranger greater leeway. You have control over the balance and the mix. You can manipulate the sounds from the various orchestral and vocal sections electronically. For television, on the other hand, you have to write strictly for the microphone. The sound is picked up once and it is funneled out into the world. There are no second takes. Consequently, your arrangement has to lean heavily on simplicity and clarity—the background has to stay out of the way of the singer. Anything that could possibly be 'misunderstood' by the mike, is left out.

"In the same way, you have to consider special conditions when you prepare an arrangement for a touring act. For one thing, you can never know what kind of musicians are going to show up for the gig in Kalamazoo. Key musicians, of course, usually travel with the act, but still you can't write the same kind of material you would for a New York recording band. You also have to consider the acoustics, which are rarely superb in the gymnasiums, auditoriums, and stadiums where a touring act performs. Again, the arranger has to keep his charts simple and crystal clear for this kind of an assignment, while at the same time generating as much excitement and freshness as the conditions allow."

Still another approach to the arranger's art is taken by Robert (Bob) Mersey.

"An arrangement," Mersey feels, "is nothing more than a tool—a vehicle that will help project a musical idea."

Mersey, who doubles as director of A. and R. for Columbia Records' pop-music division, comes by this attitude, in part, as a result of his executive responsibilities. As director of A. and R., he plays a central role in the formulation of Columbia's over-all musical policy. Consequently, he can see the arranger's contribution in the perspective of the over-all problem of musical creation.

"What is it exactly that we are selling?" Mersey asks. "When you cut down to the heart of the matter, our stock in trade boils down to nothing more than a phantom—a dream, an idea expressed in sound. Basically, this is what we are dealing with. This is what a song is, a dream the listener can identify with. Melodic value, lyric interest, harmonic structure, all these things are secondary. They mean nothing when the dream fails to project to an audience.

"This ability to project is what I look for in a performer," Mersey continues. "Projection, however, comes in all shapes and sizes. There are all kinds of people in the world with all kinds of dreams, and this is reflected in the wide range of popular musical expression. A Bobby Vinton, for example, appeals to an entirely different audience than a Barbra Streisand. Both are successful artists with unique, though different, qualities. Vinton, as I see him, gives expression to the losers of the world. His singing communicates to those people who live a cliché-ridden existence where experience is second-hand and emotions come in neat, catalogued packages. Vinton has the ability to focus on this public and give voice to a dream that these people understand and respond to. As a result, he commands the loyalty and affection of a big audience.

"Barbra Streisand, on the other hand, has an entirely different appeal. She sings to the intellectuals, the sophisticates, the Madison Avenue—not the East Village—hipster. Her singing style is intense and emotion-packed, providing her audience a momentary glimpse of deeply felt life. In addition, Barbra is a remarkable singer from a technical standpoint. She has superb natural equipment. She has complete control, a great ear, and wonderful taste. When you combine these qualities with the ability to project, you have the makings of a first-rank star.

"The one thing that Barbra and Bobby have in common is sincerity. Both are completely honest musically, and this is the single most important factor in their success. Basically, both are what they sing, their individual tastes, ideas, aspirations reflect those of the audience to whom each appeals. Both provide a voice that speaks for sizable, though different, segments of the listening public.

"So long as a singer remains true to himself, so long will he maintain rapport with his audience. I have seen too many good singers ruined by chasing after somebody else's success, by trying to be something that they were not and could never be. Popular music is nothing more than communication—a reaching out from performer to listener. The artist who can reach his audience does so because he can focus on a quality in his own being that corresponds to a similar quality in his public. There is no way I know of to fake this ability or to manufacture it. The best we can do is to recognize it when it appears and nurture it before it is trampled underfoot."

This attitude governs Mersey's approach to every aspect of popular music, from arranging to promotion. An arrangement, in his view, is a tool, a technique, not an end in itself. The end is the performance, the projection of a phantom, a dream that the listener can identify with and be moved by—hopefully, to the extent that he will go out and buy the record.

"The first thing I do when preparing a chart," Mersey says, "is decide who it is a song is aimed at. Next I try to formulate in my own mind the idea that the song is trying to express. Then I decide upon the over-all feel of the performance in terms of the lyric, melodic, and rhythmic content of the song in combination with the individual quality of the singer. Once this is accomplished, the rest is anticlimax. I spend little time on the actual writing out of a chart. I generally can put down notes as fast as I can write them."

"Popular music can never be a static form," Mersey says. "It is always changing and developing. The moving force, however, won't be found in Tin Pan Alley or the record companies. It is generated, instead, by nameless kids knocking their brains out in a thousand honky-tonks and dance halls across the country, trying to tear a sound up out of their guts that will communicate to their audiences. They break all the rules, because they never knew them in the first place. Individually considered, most of their stuff is bad, but taken together it provides the moving force that keeps popular music alive and jumping. It is the job of the arranger, of the pro, to sift through this creative eruption and pick out the musically valid themes and techniques. These the pros then polish, refine, and formalize, adding them to the living language that is popular music. Sometimes we kill it."

8 CUTTING THE RECORD

In the beginning is the song and the song is the beginning. The song is the foundation stone, the bedrock on which the popular-music industry rests. The song is the basic raw material out of which a performance is made. This is where the process starts.

Before a recording session is arranged, before rehearsals are called, before the arrangements are composed, there must be the song. Everything begins with the songwriter, who shapes a melody out of imagination and his own creative impulses. Between the composition of a song and its eventual performance and recording, however, there lies a rocky road full of unexpected pitfalls and hazards.

The first step in this circuitous journey begins with a gentleman—or a lady, as the case may be—known to the industry as a song plugger. As jobs go, this is a comparatively humble station, albeit an important one. The song plugger neither writes nor performs. He is the classic middleman operating between composer and performer. It is his responsibility to see that the song is heard—in the right places.

In order to accomplish this Herculean task, he makes the rounds patiently and endlessly. He buttonholes producers, stalks managers, corners instrumentalists, talks to cousins of cousins and friends of friends, sees anyone who might possibly advance his cause. His cause, of course, is to have his song performed.

Pitted against the humble plugger stands a mountain of songs. There are new songs and old, standards and novelties, and every one is in direct competition with the plugger's song of the moment. On his side is the edifice of the popular-music industry with its insatiable demand for new material. Singers, instrumentalists, Hollywood, Broadway, night clubs, radio and record companies swallow up material as fast as it can be produced and then demand more.

High on the priority list of the song plugger is the record producer, one of the principal actors in this creative drama. He may be an independent, producing and packaging records for his own label, or he may be associated with one of the established record companies. In either case, the primary function of the producer is the production of records.

It is his task to bring artist and material together in what may hopefully be termed wedded bliss. In order to do so, the producer must be on twenty-four-hour alert for material to fit his artists—and artists to fit his material. He must be able to recognize the appeal of a song and decide who can use it to the best advantage. Finally, the producer is charged with the supervision of the record session. It is his responsibility to see that the recorded performance comes as close to perfection as is humanly possible.

To accomplish these tasks, the producer exercises a variety of skills and capabilities, all of which are intangible. The fiddler plays his fiddle, the singer sings, the arranger arranges. In each case, individual skill and accomplishment are obvious. They can be heard and seen. The producer's stock in trade, however, is made up of such will-o'-the-wisp entities as taste, judgment, the ability to gauge a fickle public's preference, a feel for instrumental and tonal combinations, a keen diplomatic sense that will enable him to draw the best out of a temperamental performer, the faculty for staying abreast of the rapidly changing musical times.

How does one measure these qualities?

The industry has a foolproof measuring stick, one that makes no mistakes—record sales. So long as a producer turns out records that sell, he is a genius and the company cannot do enough for him. Let those sales slip, and the genius becomes the goat. The "buck" stops at the producer's desk. He takes the responsibility for success—and for failure. He has pitched his mansion right smack in the middle of Ulcer Row.

Typical of the breed is one Michael (Mike) Berniker, a producer with Columbia Records. A tall, gangling, dark-haired young man whose shirttails have a distressing tendency to creep out of his pants during the course of a record session, Mike came up through the ranks, a product of the Columbia executive training program.

Before joining Columbia in 1959, however, Berniker already had considerable experience in popular entertainment. A musician, he had studied at the Juilliard School and had also spent time as a disk jockey and as music director for an army radio station.

At Columbia, Berniker has produced records with such singing stars as Jerry Vale, Steve Lawrence, Eydie Gormé, and Barbra Streisand.

"Each one poses unique problems," says Berniker. "Every performer has a distinct style and personality, and this is what you have to work with. These qualities have to be wedded to the right material. Finding this material is an important part of the producer's job. A major part of my time is spent just listening, searching for the right song for the right singer."

Once song and singer have been decided upon, the next step in the process is the organization of a recording session. First, an arranger has to be engaged to tailor the song to the requirements of the singer. Here again the producer is central to the choice. He must be intimately familiar with the capabilities of any number of arrangers and must decide which one will best enhance a particular performance. Now, he arranges a second merger—a triangle this time, combining song, singer, and arranger.

Before the arrangements are begun there is a preliminary meeting among producer, arranger, and singer.

"At these meetings," Berniker explains, "we discuss the over-all feel of an album, the orchestration and the approach to individual songs. After that, the arranger is on his own."

Once the charts are completed, the three principals meet again. At these meetings the songs are carefully rehearsed.

Tempos are determined, phrasings are worked out, and a thorough musical preparation is made prior to the actual record session.

Meanwhile, a budget for the session is established, representing a further compromise—this time between the funds available and artistic dictates.

"Every singer wants fifteen strings behind him in the band," Berniker shrugs. "The arranger wants twenty-five and I would love to have fifty. We compromise. We settle for twelve."

The next step involves the scheduling of the session. Columbia maintains several recording studios in New York as well as additional facilities in Nashville and Hollywood. One of their finest studios, however, is housed in what was once a church on East Thirtieth Street in New York. The high ceilings, wooden roof, and spacious floor make for excellent acoustics; add the most modern recording equipment available and you have something that comes close to being the ideal studio.

Once the date is established, the arranger, who will also conduct the session, alerts his contractor to hire the band. The contractor's principal function rests in his possession of an important list of names. These are musicians who have demonstrated the ability to enhance a record session and who can be expected to do the same for this specific job.

In the past, name bands did most of the commercial recordings. Today, however, the name band is practically extinct. Ninety-nine per cent of all records, singles and albums, are made by pick-up orchestras that come together only to play a particular recording. It is the contractor's job to bring them together and to administer the complicated paperwork in relation to taxes, welfare and pension plans, and union regulations.

Mel Tax, a saxophone player who doubles on the clarinet and flute, has established a niche in this rank of contractors. A lifelong musician, Mel has run the gamut of professional experience. At one time or another he has been a staff musician for a radio station, played club dates, night clubs, Broadway shows, and concerts.

Mel's principal concern is the quality of the band he assembles for the session. Actually, this concern is somewhat academic. The level of competence on his extensive list of musicians is downright awesome. In a big recording center like New York City, the comparatively highly paid record industry attracts the best, and the best is superb.

Mel's favorite concertmaster, for example, is George Ockner—a violinist who has probably been heard by more people than any other in history, even though few people outside of the industry know his name. When you hear a silky violin obbligato, superbly phrased and articulated, sounded discreetly under a singer, chances are that you are listening to George. Short, balding, with a wry sense of humor and an unassuming manner, Ockner brings to his work a concert-caliber technique, an exquisite tone, and the authority that comes with thirty years of experience and thorough academic training.

Seated alongside Ockner at the session may be such other outstanding violinists as David Nadien, now concertmaster of the New York Philharmonic; Arnold Eidus, who made his concert debut in New York's Town Hall when he was eleven years old; Tascha Samaroff, a dapper, cigar-smoking violinist who toured the world as a child prodigy; or Matthew Raimondi, concertmaster for many of the chamber orchestras that play in New York. Among them, they might share a quarter of a million dollars' worth of violins, including examples by Stradivarius, Guarnerius, Bergonzi, and other Italian masters.

Once the band has been engaged and the session scheduled, the next step involves the studio. Here the recording engineer is king. He sets up the microphones, balances the sounds from the different orchestra sections, arranges the seating, and assumes the responsibility for getting as true and precise a record of the sounds generated by this talented coterie on tape as is electronically possible.

Frank Laico of Columbia Records is considered a past master at this game. He has been with Columbia since 1939 and has witnessed a major technological revolution. When he began, master records were cut in a shellac disk. Today, Frank manipulates a complicated panel that controls an eight-track stereo system fed by as many as twenty individual microphones.

Each one of these microphones presents its own problem. Each has to be placed so as to best pick up the sound of a particular section or a certain musician. At the same time, leakage—sound from one section being picked up by the microphone from another—must be kept to a minimum.

"Actually," Frank explains, "there is no set rule or formula for placing the various sections or their microphones. It really boils down to experience and judgment—a question of personal preference. The engineer's job is to get a sound that is as close to reality as is possible. That is the important thing. If it helped, we would put the musicians on the ceiling."

A typical seating arrangement for a record session might be as follows: brass, woodwinds, and strings are individually grouped and separated from each other by large, movable sound baffles. The percussion section—drums, bass, guitars, and piano—each has its own microphone pickup and the different instruments are generally isolated from one another by baffles. The chorus has its own cubicle and microphone, as does the singer. In the middle of all this is the arranger, who conducts the session. Conductor, drummer, and, on occasion, bass player and guitarists are equipped with earphones that carry the lead singer's voice. This additional precaution is necessary because these people must be able to hear the singer in order to make the subtle shifts in rhythm necessary to follow the singer's style. The rest of the band follows the rhythm sections.

Once the band is engaged, the studio reserved, the seating arrangements completed, and the microphones set up, the session is ready to begin. This is the moment of truth. Hopefully, this collection of talent has been brought together to create a record that will find favor with the public. To accomplish this end, a staggering level of competence is focused on the problem—a level we would hope to find in a hospital operating theater. Everything is geared to ease the task of the featured artist. He, or she, is confident that the full support of band, arranger, engineer, producer is marshaled to this end.

The singer has already gone over the songs to be recorded with the arranger and producer. He knows the tempos, the general turn of phrasing and is familiar with the over-all feel of the arrangements. In the preliminary rehearsals, the three principals have already established the musical outlines of the session.

The musicians in the band (in industry parlance, it is always a band, never an orchestra) sit down cold. They have never seen the music which, more often than not, arrives from the copyist at the last minute. They are expected to sit down and after a reading or two, during which time any mistakes in the chart are ironed out, give a letter-perfect performance. They rarely fall short of this expectation. Not even when last-minute changes are made. A singer, for example, may decide that he will feel more comfortable a half-note higher or lower than what is written in the score. In such a case, which happens more often than one would think, the musicians must transpose the music they have just seen and play it in accordance with the desire of the singer.

Then again, the sound of a particular musical configuration may not coincide with what the arranger, producer, or singer had in mind. Modifications are made on the spot. A passage may be eliminated from the strings, or an additional passage written in for the woodwinds. During this preliminary rehearsal, adjustments are also made by the sound engineer. He wanders about the studio adjusting microphones, moving players, erecting an additional sound baffle where he feels it will be needed, and generally arranging things for optimum results.

The atmosphere in the studio is genial and relaxed. Everyone concerned is confident that he will perform professionally and more, that his competence will be equal to any contingency that may occur at the session. There is humorous banter about the mistakes that creep into the charts and a running commentary by the musicians as the kinks are ironed out.

The scene arranges itself. The singer, if he is young or

so constituted, will have his own entourage at the session—managers, friends, and relatives who constitute a cheering section that will spur him on to greater accomplishments. The old pros dispense with this kind of psychological aid, relying instead on a stiff belt of scotch. The producer is worried, but manages to disguise his state with a show of unassailable confidence. The arranger is curious to see how his charts are going to sound. The musicians are cool, acting as though the exhibition of even the smallest spark of enthusiasm will cost them their union cards.

Finally, everything is ready. The producer, ensconced in the control booth, announces the call letters that identify a particular song for the session. His voice blares into the studio through a loudspeaker: "CL 6-1719 S 'Nothing But Love.' Take one."

A red light, signifying that the recording machines are in operation, flashes on and the arranger gives the beat. "A-one, a-two, a-one, two, three, ——"; the last beat is left silent so that the conductor's voice will not leak into the opening chord—and the band plays.

Now, a remarkable transformation in atmosphere occurs. The banter and jokes are forgotten as everyone in the studio concentrates on the task at hand. No extraneous sounds are made as the music pours from instruments and throats, picked up by the all-hearing microphones. Suddenly, the pattern is broken. The voice of the producer intrudes through the loudspeaker. The band dissolves in a hideous discord.

Something went wrong. If it was in the band, a sloppy entrance or a wrong note (a "clam" in the vernacular), the producer explains through the loudspeaker. More often, the singer flubbed an entrance or garbled a word. In that case, the producer rushes out of the control booth and has a hurried, whispered conference with the singer. Back in the booth, he identifies the next take: "CL 6-1719 S 'Nothing But Love'. Take two."

Once more the red warning light flashes on, the band becomes silent and the conductor begins again. "a-one, a-two, a-one, two, three, ——."

This process is repeated any number of times until the producer feels he has enough material in the can with which to fashion a finished record. The taping process provides considerable leeway because sections from a number of different takes can be cut and spliced together to make the finished product.

Occasionally, the producer, singer, or arranger will ask to hear a particular take. When this happens, the musicians relax. They get up from their desks, make phone calls to their answering services, and discuss—in order of preference —families, homes, sporting events, instruments, and funny incidents that occurred in past recording sessions.

A record session is organized around a three-hour time limit, established by the musicians' union. During this period an average of five or six songs will be recorded. On occasion the session runs overtime—a cause for celebration among the musicians and a gnashing of teeth for the producer, who is responsible for keeping the session within a prescribed budget. Overtime is expensive and is always avoided if possible. Most sessions end in a last-minute race with the clock.

Once the five or six songs scheduled for the session are in the can, the process is finished as far as the musicians and arranger are concerned. The material on tape, however, is still far from the finished product that will eventually find its way into record stores and onto radio programs. The sounds recorded at the session represent the raw material out of which the finished record will be processed. This finishing stage is done in an editing booth by the producer.

"This is probably the most personally creative aspect of the producer's job," says Mike Berniker. "We juggle the component parts taped at the session until we come up with something we feel is polished and appealing."

This juggling can be extensive. The various sections of the band are individually taped, with some leakage from other sections, and can be technically manipulated at the will of the editor. A section can be brought up into prominence or merged into the over-all background sound. Different instruments may be featured or the sound of a whole section may be subjected to electronic modifications.

The lead singing voice is also subject to modification in the editing booth. On occasion, the voice may be over-dubbed at different pitch levels. The result is the voice of the singer heard in a three-part harmony performed with uncannily precise ensemble.

The extent of modification that can be made in the editing room are practically endless and represent a vital step in the over-all production of a record. Some producers consider this the single most important aspect of the creation of a good record.

After the session has been recorded, the tapes edited and a master patched together, the record now passes from A. and R. into Sales Promotion. Here on in, the record becomes the responsibility of the promoters—but that is another story.

The art inherent in the history and mythology of America were also denied the Negro slave, though for a different reason. History is art to the extent, at least, that it is colored and modified by the wish-factor in the population of a particular country. The history of America, for example, is very different when it is taught in England or the Soviet Union from the history that is taught to children in America.

The high-sounding slogans, the larger-than-life heroes that Americans revere, had a hollow ring in the ear of the slave. How could he, for example, venerate the memory of a George Washington or a Thomas Jefferson when he knew that for all their vaunted morality, for all their ringing pronouncements, they were parties to the most unjust and immoral relationship that a person can enter into—that of owning slaves? They bought and sold human beings and exploited their labor. The attitude of the Negro slave toward the traditions and myths of American history was different from that of the slave master.

This attitude was reflected by the late Negro poet Langston Hughes, who wrote:

> Let's make America America again
> Not that it ever was

The American Negro, then, was left with only two channels into which to funnel his creative energies—music and religion—in both of which he has made significant advances, producing a Charlie Parker in one area and a Martin Luther King in the other.

Music, basically, needs no more than the exercise of the human body. Almost everyone can sing and clap his hands or beat his feet, thereby providing the two fundamentals of music—rhythm and melody. Even leisure time is not necessary. One can sing while working. Indeed, hard work is made easier by singing.

Although his cultural heritage and traditions were systematically obliterated by the slave master, the Negro retained the memory of a rich musical tradition. This retention revealed itself in the modifications the Negro made on European secular and religious music. It was demonstrated in a special type of singing, in the call-and-response pattern of the work song, in the supple harmonies of the spiritual. Musicologists have traced this retention directly to the musical forms and styles of West Africa, the region from which most American Negroes originally came.

Severely limited in his aspirations by a cruel and immoral social situation, the exploited and despised black man turned to music. His creative energies were funneled into and focused on this one area. It is not surprising, then, that the Negro demonstrated marked musicality.

Not only were his inherent musical abilities highlighted in this manner, but his selective capabilities were also sharpened and enhanced. The Negro slave came to music in an innocent state, innocent in the sense that music for him served a purely creative function. He did not need to be influenced by any snobbish or national appeal, nor could he consider music an individual adornment—a cultural attainment with which to impress his neighbors. For him music was a question of survival, music was a collective expression in which the entire community participated. It was solace and inspiration—that art, which above all others made the life of the slave bearable.

The musicality of the Negro was evident from the first introduction of slaves into the New World. In fact, it was noted by no less a personage than Thomas Jefferson, who wrote in his *Notes on Virginia:* "In music they [Negroes] are more generally gifted than the whites, with accurate ears for tune and time, and they have been found capable of imagining a small catch."

This "small catch" was destined to have a deeper influence on subsequent musical development than Jefferson, reflecting the racist opinion of his time, ever dreamed possible.

It is interesting to note that the music of the American Indian has left little imprint upon the musical development of the New World. Yet the Indian was as musically gifted as any other man and music played a more prominent role in his social and tribal life than it did in European life. The absence of an Indian influence can best be explained by the fact that Indian music was totally different from that of Europe or Africa. Musically, the American Indian and the European were as far apart as they were geographically. Rhythmic, melodic, and harmonic structures of the two musics were completely alien.

African music, on the other hand, is more closely related to European music. The diatonic scale, for example, is common to both, and forms the strongest link between them as well as the mark that distinguishes them from all other musical systems. Then there is the basic concept of harmony shared by African and European music, though this factor was more highly developed in the European tradition.

The African conception of rhythm, however, is more complex and sophisticated than the European. In European music different rhythms, as a rule, may be employed successively, but rarely simultaneously. A characteristic of African music, however, is just this simultaneous utilization of different rhythmic patterns.

A typical example may utilize three, sometimes four or

five, different rhythmic patterns in one musical statement. A common combination, still in use all over West Africa, has two percussion parts, one of which may be the clapping of hands or the beating of feet, against a vocal section with its own rhythmic pattern. Often, in more formal performance, there are several metrical patterns in percussion, each played by a drum of different size and tonal timbre. Chaos is avoided by the presence of an underlying beat that never varies. Rhythm in African music is conceived of as a combination of different time patterns that coincide at regular intervals. This underlying beat is also characteristic of European music.

These considerations, which were exhaustively studied by the musicologists Kolinski and Watermann, reveal the factors common to both African and European music. These factors, in turn, facilitate the process of musical synthesis, or blending, when the two musical systems are brought into contact with each other over a period of time. This is exactly what happened in America and explains the homogeneous character of American Negro music.

This relationship between the African and European musical traditions was eloquently demonstrated on a recent television program by the folk singer Pete Seeger. In discussing African influence on American music, he sang a traditional Irish fiddle reel. Then he sang a modification of the same tune as it was utilized in a Louisiana Negro field song. In the modification, the lilting Irish tune was expressed in a syncopated rhythmic extension, swinging to a definite ragtime beat.

The Negro, then, acted as a musical catalyst. He borrowed from the music he heard around him, from Protestant hymns as well as secular songs and dances. Because of his innocence, he was able to select those aspects that had intrinsic musical value. This music, in turn, was enriched by his own African heritage, and the whole mélange was perfected and enhanced by a severely restricted creative energy. In the crucible of the slave warren, musical gold was being refined. It was not long before others recognized its value.

This influence was recognized as early as 1753, as can be seen in a description of a Richmond ball that was printed in *The Virginia Gazette*. The account, after listing the notables who attended the affair, went on to comment upon the music of Sy Gilliat and London Brigs, two Negro musicians who acted as official entertainers at state balls. Gilliat played the violin and Brigs played the flute. Both were the "property" of Baron Botetourt, later Governor General of the Virginia colony. The potency of their music was described like this:

> . . . to the music of Gilliat's fiddle and Brig's flute, all sorts of capers were cut. . . . Sometimes a "congo" was danced and when the music grew fast and furious a jig climaxed the evening. . . .

This mention of the congo as a social dance in colonial Virginia is significant. The congo, which was described by Lafcadio Hearn more than a hundred years later after seeing it danced by Negroes in New Orleans in 1858, was nothing more than a modified version of an African tribal dance that was performed by Negroes throughout the eighteenth and nineteenth centuries all over the New World. It is interesting to note that a version was also performed by the dandies of colonial Virginia society.

By the beginning of the nineteenth century, this influence, which was only hinted at in this eighteenth-century account, became obvious. Its first really national expression, however, came with the immensely popular minstrel show, which, as we have seen, dominated American popular music throughout the nineteenth century and was applauded enthusiastically throughout most of the rest of the world as well.

Negro music in America evolved in two distinct phases whose roots can be traced to the colonial period. One phase developed out of secular music—a synthesis of Scotch-Irish, English, German, and French songs and dances that were transformed and enriched by the introduction of an African heritage.

This line of development can be traced from plantation songs to the minstrel show, then through ragtime and on into jazz. All along this line of development additions and modifications were constantly being made to the original source. These came about through the requirements of the popular stage and commercial considerations as well as through technical considerations that involved instruments and, much later, recording techniques.

Many of these developments and modifications were the result of the activities of white musicians and performers. The source, however, is unmistakably Negro, and this influence is plainly distinguishable in the work of such white composers as Stephen Foster, George Gershwin, Irving Berlin, and Richard Rodgers.

The second phase of this musical development evolved around the activities of the church. The synthesis of African traditions with Protestant hymns gave birth to the spiritual, with all of its ramifications in the development of the blues, jazz, and Negro gospel singing.

Again, we can trace a line of development that runs from

the West African call-and-response chant to American Negro work songs and field hollers, to the spiritual, to gospel singing, and finally, to today's rock-and-roll. If jazz can be considered the secular expression of the American Negro, then rock-and-roll must be considered an expression of his religious life—an echo of that "joyous shout unto the Lord" voiced by the indomitable spirit of a sorely oppressed and abused people.

Another line of musical development which has had a marked influence on American popular music also derives from the experience of the Negro. This genesis, however, took place in South America and the Caribbean islands, notably Cuba and Jamaica, and is popularly known today as Latin-American music.

Evolving under similar conditions, this music is the result of a synthesis of African with Spanish and Portuguese traditions. American popular music represents a blend of African with primarily Anglo-Saxon traditions. The fact that both Afro-Cuban and Latin American music found such a ready audience in North America can be attributed to this common base, and we have seen how Latin American rhythms influenced the development of jazz in turn-of-the-century New Orleans.

This music created by the Negroes of North and South America has won an audience throughout the world. Jazz, swing, the rhumba and the samba, and rock-and-roll are now in the mainstream of popular music in practically every country. All of these forms owe their peculiar vitality and inventiveness to the Negro musical genius.

Their music represents a cultural contribution of the first order. All over the world, wherever people come together for relaxation and pleasure, an unrecognized partner in the festivities is the Negro of the Americas. It is his songs we sing and his rhythms we dance to.

This is a music that has been some three hundred years in the making. A music that was once a question of life and death—nothing less. To understand this fact, we must go back to the Negro slaves who brought this music to the Americas. Over a period of three hundred years of the slave trade, an estimated sixteen to twenty million died in the passage from Africa, and the survivors who reached these shores were as close to being dead as any forcibly transported people in history.

All this dying was bad for business. A live slave was a negotiable asset; a dead one was worthless. The slave traders, being practical men, tried to reduce this disastrous mortality rate. They gave the slaves good red beans to eat and clean water to drink. Sometimes they gave them better living quarters than those of the crew, but still the Negroes insisted on dying.

Then someone discovered that if you made slaves sing and dance they stayed alive. Just plain exercise was no good. It had to be the lindy, the rhumba and the twist, only the real originals of these dances. It was this factor that led Thomas Starks, a London merchant in the slave trade, to write the captain of the bark *Africa* in 1700, which had taken on a cargo of 450 slaves from the Gold Coast: "Make your Negroes cheerful and pleasant, making them dance at the beating of the drum. . . ."

It is this music, modified and altered through countless evolutions, that we still listen and respond to. It gave birth to ragtime and jazz, to the rhumba and the samba, to gospel song and rock-and-roll. It represents the single most significant cultural contribution made by any minority group. The Negro taught America how to sing and dance, and today the whole world has taken up his beat.

INDEX

155